# Percy
# Grainger

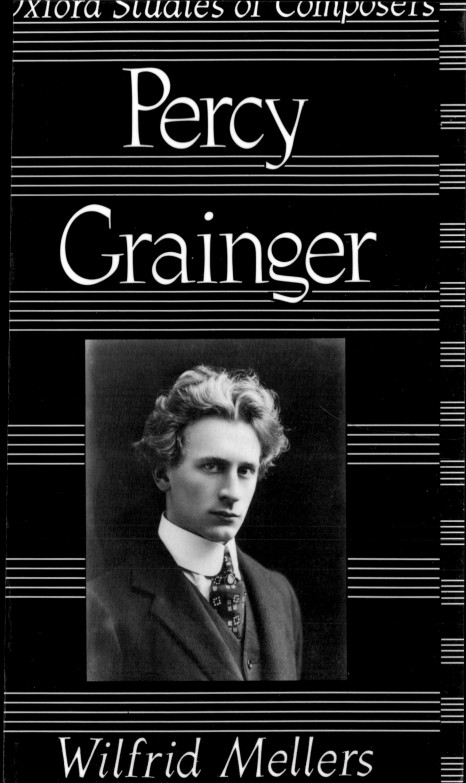

*Wilfrid Mellers*

# PERCY GRAINGER

*Oxford Studies of Composers*

# PERCY GRAINGER

## WILFRID MELLERS

Oxford   New York
OXFORD UNIVERSITY PRESS

Oxford University Press, Walton Street, Oxford OX2 6DP
Oxford New York Toronto
Delhi Bombay Calcutta Madras Karachi
Kuala Lumpur Singapore Hong Kong Tokyo
Nairobi Dar es Salaam Cape Town
Melbourne Auckland
and associated companies in
Berlin Ibadan Madrid

Oxford is a trade mark of Oxford University Press

Published in the United States
by Oxford University Press Inc., New York

British Library Cataloguing in Publication Data
(Data available)
ISBN 0–19–816269–3
ISBN 0–19–816270–7 (Pbk)

Library of Congress Cataloging in Publication Data
Mellers, Wilfrid Howard, 1914–
Percy Grainger / Wilfrid Mellers.—
(Oxford studies of composers)
Includes bibliographical references.
1. Grainger, Percy, 1882–1961. 2. Composers—Biography.
I. Title. II. Series.
ML410.G75M4 1992        786.2'092–dc20
ISBN 0–19–816269–3 (cloth):
ISBN 0–19–816270–7 (paper)

2 4 6 8 10 9 7 5 3

Set by Hope Services (Abingdon) Ltd.,
Printed in Great Britain by
Biddles Ltd, Guildford and King's Lynn

To
John Paynter,
another musical maker and activator

# ACKNOWLEDGEMENTS

My main debts are to Jane Allen for secretarial help; to John Paynter, for reading and editing the typescript; and to Barry Peter Ould, secretary and music archivist of the Percy Grainger Society, who has been unfailingly supportive and generous in the provision of scores and advice. But for his help, I'd have found it difficult, perhaps impossible, to chart a way through the chaotic seas of Grainger's projects and publications. During the early stages of the book's gestation, I also owed much to Kay Dreyfus, one-time curator of the Grainger Museum in Melbourne. On a recent visit to Australia, I talked with her at some length; and profited from biographical and musical material she put in my way. I enjoyed talking to Therese Radic whilst in Melbourne; and found her play *A Whip Round for Percy Grainger* (which I read but didn't see produced) both illuminating and amusing.

Kay Dreyfus is the editor of the Grainger letters, published by Macmillan under the title of *The Farthest North of Humanness*. All my quotations from Grainger's letters come from this volume. The quotations from his public rather than private writings are from *A Musical Genius from Australia: Selected Writings by and about Percy Grainger*, compiled and with commentary by Teresa Balough, a monograph published by the University of Western Australia Music Department. I have also made use of John Blacking's *A Commonsense View of all Music*, an enquiry into the nature and potential of ethnomusicology, triggered off by a series of quotations from Grainger's spasmodically stimulating hunches, rather than theories or thoughts. John Bird's fine biography, enthusiastically sympathetic yet critically balanced, has been, of course, a necessary stand-by. My small book concentrates on the music rather than the man: though the unusual nature of Grainger's musical achievement depends on his being so paradoxical a person.

2 May 1991

# CONTENTS

Of course I am a mixture. I need both contrasts. I could hardly have stayed much longer happily in England . . . I felt a great need to see the old old hot places again and to hear the silly Australian speech and to bask in the holy pure virgin landscapes.

My child dreams in Australia, my boy dreams in Germany, my young man's plans in early London: I can't forget any of them thoroughly and each one that fails of fulfilment will have a black mark against it in my painstaking hardworking memory . . . My manifold amateurish interests lead me to myriads of graves that other fellow talents never tread. The whole being of folk art is closely akin to all or many racial and artistic burials. Dead ideas, words, myths, plots, occupations flit about through the dying rhymes. And folksingers too: in them I'm hoarding up a wealth of dead friends soon to go. All the languages I potter about with are hornets nests of new births and old deaths, full of wistful suggestions to the loving and sympathetic mind. I always see both sides. I grieve with the Irish for what griefs the English saddled them and I mourn with the English for all the troubles the silly Irish have been to them.

My own compositions I undertake largely as a kind of life insurance against my coming death. Let there be no records wanting, of any folk, language, song history, not even of myself: perhaps least of all of myself.

(Percy Grainger, letter to Karen Holten, 2 July 1909)


In thinking of me, try to remember these things: I was born right—I don't have to 'develop'. I am happy thru and thru: happy in my race, happy in my art . . . I don't care a straw about god and eternity because I am quite complete as I am. I don't have to behave morally—I am good. In other words, I am an Australian.

(Percy Grainger, letter to Alfhild Sandby, 30 March 1940)

# LIST OF MUSIC EXAMPLES

# PRELUDE

## *The Importance of being Percy*

Many, perhaps most, of the monographs in this series have been devoted to composers whose work is not well known to the general public. There are exceptions, for the series includes a book on that familiar mover and shaker Debussy, and one on Messiaen, of whom most musical people are at least aware. On the whole, however, the series has directed attention to composers, such as Dunstable, Carissimi, Sweelinck, and Schoenberg, whose historical significance, and perhaps 'greatness', is indubitable though their music is not widely disseminated. That applies even to Lassus, a climactic figure in Europe's late Renaissance, whose work is still not readily available to the man in the street. Of course, historical figures may gravitate into the ranks of the great, as has happened over the last fifteen years to Marc-Antoine Charpentier, the seventeenth-century French composer now far more comprehensively recorded, and even concert-performed, than his (in his own day more esteemed) contemporary Lully, and appropriately the subject of a recent addition to the Oxford Studies of Composers.

Percy Grainger, in such company, is an anomaly. He is not a great composer on any count, and is not historically significant in the sense that Dunstable, Carissimi, or Schoenberg is. Yet he occupies a peculiar, possibly important, position in the story of twentieth-century culture, if not of music itself. Most people know him as the composer of lollipops for piano, wind-band, or theatre orchestra, of which the most ubiquitous is *Country Gardens* (1908). Although he lived comfortably off these pieces for much of his longish life, Grainger deprecated their popularity because it distracted attention from what he considered to be more significant achievements. His crossness may have been unjustified in that, on the evidence of his 'serious' works, he wasn't anything approaching a major composer; but his displeasure had validity in so far as he was a phenomenon the import of which has been only recently recognized.

I

Born on 8 July 1882 at Brighton, Victoria, in far Australia, Grainger was a composer of the Global Village, remembering that 'folk' traditionally live in villages. His father was an architect from London, his mother the daughter of a London hotelier, now resident in Adelaide, Australia. The father, John Harry Grainger, dabbled in the arts of literature, painting, and music and was certainly not the disreputable alcoholic Percy later painted him as. He was, however, too addicted to wine and women; and infected his wife with the syphilis that may have had some bearing on her nervous and physical disabilities. Percy's dismissal of him was hardly surprising, especially since he was more often absent than present. Left much in the company of his formidable mother, Rose Aldridge, Percy was doted on, perhaps on the far side of idolatry. Reluctant to let her beautiful son out of her sight, Rose took him away from his Melbourne state school after a mere three months, and herself tutored him at home, feeding him on Anglo-Saxon chronicles and Icelandic sagas and sowing in him the seeds of his slightly lunatic dislike of people with brown eyes and dark hair. Later Percy absorbed this into a paranoid hatred of European classical (Greek and Roman) culture, and into a rejection of the reigning Austro-German hegemony in music: not without some inconsistency, since German culture could be and was appropriated to his Nordic fervour if occasion offered or necessitated. John Grainger was by no means insensitive to his son's childish charms ('You would so like to see him', he wrote on 4 January 1890, 'fair, very fair, with long, curling golden hair, blue eyes, and legs fit to carry the Tower of Babel'). But John was no match for Rose's idolatry, and scarcely shared her life, let alone her bed, after Percy was born. Indeed, the parents separated in the very year in which John had paid that starry-eyed tribute to Percy's beauty. From the age of 8, the boy was in Rose's sole company and control. That he should have grown up odd is hardly surprising, though his charms proved on the whole stronger than his neuroses.

The liveliness of his mind and his artistic abilities were early manifest. Rose, who was widely if erratically read and a fair musician, taught him what he most needed to know, and gave him piano lessons from the age of 5 to 10: in which climactic year he discovered the principle of what he was later to call Free Music, was inspired to the point of obsession by Grettir and the Nordic heroes, and discovered the overwhelming significance (for him) of the music of Bach! Rose unsurprisingly found him a handful and sent him to study with Louis Pabst, a one-time pupil of Rubinstein. Such was Percy's keyboard precocity that in July 1894, aged 12, he gave a glamorous debut recital at Melbourne's Masonic Hall. Other 'benefit' recitals raised funds that enabled Rose to take him to study in Frankfurt am Main, for Germany was still the accredited home of musical culture. Between 1895 and 1899 he was coached at the Hoch Conservatorium by James Kwast on piano and by Ivan Knorr in harmony and counterpoint. Though quickly assimilative, Percy did not take kindly to an academic curriculum. He responded readily, however, to the European milieu, and especially to Karl Klimsch, a lithographer and talented amateur musician who had the nous to see what Percy needed in musical terms, and who encouraged his far from negligible gifts as a visual artist. Moreover, the conservatorium offered the stimulation of musical companions, if not of enterprising instruction. Percy teamed up with a group of young Britishers, Roger Quilter, Balfour Gardiner, Norman O'Neill, and Cyril Scott. It may not be an accident that the reputations of Quilter especially, and to a lesser degree of Balfour Gardiner and O'Neill, survive as composers of 'light' music. Cyril Scott, the big gun among them, although now almost forgotten, enjoyed, in the first two decades of the century, an immense and not merely local celebrity. Reading Percy's letters we are recurrently taken aback by the consistency with which, bewailing the stuffiness of the musical establishment, he applauds the truly creative innovators of his time—Debussy, Ravel, Stravinsky, Bartók, Schoenberg, Busoni—and Cyril Scott! One must accept the fact that time does its winnowing with impartiality, but must pay homage to Scott who, whatever the value of his music, was a man of integrity, imagination, and high intelligence—and perhaps the only one among Percy's contemporaries who understood the nature of his genius. Scott's essay on Grainger, published in the *Musical Quarterly* in 1916, is still one of the most insightful explorations of why and how Grainger matters.

Scott would have understood what Grainger was on about when, late in life, he claimed that he had gone to study in Germany because the German language was close to Icelandic, in which his beloved sagas had been written. In fact, of course, Rose took him to Germany because that was where any parent, considerate of a musical child's future, would have taken him. There he was reared on the German (Brahmsian) techniques which were the staple diet of a serious European musician of his generation; and the craftsmanship he acquired was no less useful because he had to unlearn some of it when he discovered the true nature of his talents. He was confused about the unlearning process too, maintaining that he knew nothing of folk-song until, in 1905, he heard Lucy Broadwood's famous lecture 'On Collecting English Folksongs', joined the English Folksong Society himself, and embarked, with the help of his wax-cylinder phonograph, on field-work in Lincolnshire. In fact, he had made a series of folk-song arrangements for voice and piano as early as 1898, and two years later had produced fourteen short settings of Songs of the North. Still, it was true that the inspirational Lucy Broadwood revealed what folk-song might mean to him, and encouraged him in field-work both more intuitively imaginative and more scientific in method than any previously undertaken in Britain. During his student days in Frankfurt he was not only unaware of this potential, but was busy developing his gifts as a virtuoso pianist, an area wherein he earned early success outstripping that of his first ventures into composition, youthfully inventive though some of them were.

His student days over, Percy had moved in 1901, of course with Rose, to London, to make his living as a concert pianist who tickled the ears of the aristocracy and the industrial *nouveau riche*. London also served as a base for concert tours; and his money-making capacity mattered more when Rose, undergoing the first of a series of nervous disorders, was less able to contribute to their support by teaching English. Soon established as a 'giant' of the keyboard, Percy was especially esteemed for his performances of Bach and Schumann, though he didn't favour the central Viennese tradition from Haydn to Beethoven, the latter being almost his *bête noire*. As pianist, Grainger was a showman who pre-sented—made present—the past, and who loved to play the music of his own time with which he empathized. This included 'moderns' like Debussy, Ravel, and the Albéniz of *Iberia*, but above all it meant his own music and that of Grieg, of whose Piano Concerto he gave performances that became legendary. Fortunately, he was blessed with the physical energy that enabled him to make gladiatorial progress through 'Nordic' Russia, Scandinavia, Ireland, Holland, and Germany, as well as South Africa and his native Australasia. Private relationships sprouted from his arduous public life; he met and delighted in Grieg and Delius, whose music meant so much to him, and between 1905 and 1908 managed to embrace his busiest period of folk-song exploration into his strenuous professional schedule. The folk-song collecting bore more potently on his future destiny than he or the slightly grudging Rose—who thought he should devote more time to his 'own' music—realized.

For Percy was a composer of paradox whose aboriginal compositions were to prove neither his best nor his most original. His juvenile and adolescent works may fascinate in their vernal attempts (in Ezra Pound's phrase) to Make It New; yet as achieved art they don't wear as well as the music he 'dished up' from communal and folk sources. That the bulk of Grainger's music is not original composition but arrangements of or rambles around traditional material proves to be a consequence not of deficient invention, but rather of the fact that for Grainger, as a Global Village composer, old worlds had to be reborn, in the process making it new far more convincingly than had the young man's deliberate exercises in modernity. Even the more neurasthenic contrarieties of human passion, which crop up in Grainger's usually ebullient originals, may be annealed in being absorbed into communal experience: in which context even the loneliest loner need not be totally alone. The authenticity of Grainger's folk-song settings, we'll discover, lies precisely in their apparent non-authenticity: for in them old tales and ballads are re-enacted in a manner closer to ritual festivity than to concert performance, so that they become valid now, as they had been then. In the long run Grainger wasn't trying to be an 'art' composer in the European sense; he was rather a maker and activator who sundered barriers between aural-oral and literate traditions, and between the genres we arbitrarily call art, folk, and pop.

In 1914 Rose again broke down, and the First World War broke out: coincident events that encouraged the Graingers to migrate to America. Percy disingenuously admitted that, since he hoped to be the first Australian composer of consequence, he disliked the notion of dying in a war he considered idiotic. He continued to pursue his career as a virtuoso pianist, at least until the United States entered the war in 1916. He did not, however, declare himself a conscientious objector; and through sundry musical contacts found an appropriate niche as an instructor in the Fifteenth Band of the Coast Artillery Corps: a move that influenced his career significantly, if less decisively than his earlier espousal of folk music. For as a bandsman Grainger acquired an expert knowledge of wind instruments, by which he'd been fascinated since the turn of the century, and became adept at scoring and composing for them. A substantial proportion of the music he composed during his American years—virtually from 1914 until the end of his life—involved the American military or collegiate band, and his largest work for these forces, *A Lincolnshire Posy*, has claims to being considered his masterpiece.

In 1918, when the war ended, Percy became an American citizen, and three years later settled at White Plains, New York, which was to be his permanent home. The move to White Plains proved, however, traumatic, for Rose's nervous and physical disabilities grew rapidly more desperate until, in 1922, she committed suicide. The immediate trigger to this act seems to have been rumours circulated by one of Percy's girl-friends that the relation between the mother and son was incestuous. Though it almost certainly wasn't, there can be no doubt that Rose's Mother Love released very dark forces. Not only did she mercilessly torment any young woman who was or even might be Percy's lover, she also 'tested' her son's devotion by moral blackmail of fiendish ingenuity, to the point of shamming dead. Yet not even Rose's physical decease could efface what Percy called 'The Together-Life of Rose and Percy Grainger', this being his first memorial tribute to her, soon to be followed by a seventy-five page 'Life of my Mother and her Son', and by a picture-book of 'Photos of Rose Grainger, and of three Short Accounts of her Life by Herself'. That the relationship of this mother and son—who appropriated her maiden name of Aldridge into all his published compositions—was to a degree pathological can hardly be doubted. She arrested him in childhood, if not infantilism, and was certainly in part responsible for his sado-masochistic proclivities. Rose, knowing about them, disapproved: though not so much as she disapproved of rivals for his affections, especially the delightful Dane, Karen Holten. With Karen, Grainger corresponded voluminously and frankly, since Rose did all she could to prevent their meeting. In 1906 Percy proclaimed to Karen that, 'I stand for everything that is democratic and irreligious, ignore all *value*, don't believe in the existence of *soul* in either man or woman, and since bodiliness is to me the highest aim, rate woman (if anything) higher than man'. Although it seems improbable that

Karen fully shared in Percy's relish of their flagellatory capers, she tolerated them because she found so much in his charm, vivacity, and generosity of spirit to love and revere; while Percy was at least able to admit that although (alas) she didn't have blue eyes, she had a 'blue-eyed heart'. Given that, he could exclaim, 'I am in love with you, in my way, and so deeply grateful and happy to have you, only not as a married husband but as a free childish ridiculous lover'. Still closer on the mark, however, were the words he addressed to Rose in 1910: 'I not only love you I don't know how much, but what is of quite an other weight, you are my particular and ONLY LIFE'S COMRADE, were always so, and will be "till death do us part".'

John Bird, in his masterly biography of Grainger, doesn't gloss over Rose's pathological condition, and commits himself to the—as he admits, clinically improbable—assertion that 'Percy Grainger was mad'. Whatever the case, Grainger's mental state is only indirectly relevant to a book about his music; and although, as we examine that music, we'll discover that both its nature and its limitations were conditioned by the oddities of his psyche, all that matters is what, being as he was, he created, not what he might have created, had he been different. All his friends had deplored his passivity in the face of Rose's monstrous domination; yet Percy considered it 'unbelievable that anyone should live for love (or passion) in defiance of a mother's wish . . . I have taken love action only when advised to do so by my mother. Any other thought is sickeningly repugnant to me.' Even so, Percy had his own moral courage. Against the odds, he recovered from Rose's death, and in 1925 met Ella Ström, a blonde Swede of 37 who physically resembled Rose. With his mother safely dead and buried, Percy married Ella in 1928, and on the whole the marriage worked. Ella was an amateur painter and a writer of (bad) light verse: not a very intelligent woman, but beautiful, sensual, sexually experienced, and self-confident. Though the marriage was hardly easy, it survived, notwithstanding Percy's abnormalities, until his death thirty-three years later.

From their home at White Plains the Graingers made sporadic forays to Scandinavia to collect folk-songs and to visit their extensive circle of friends. The collection of Danish songs he assembled between 1925 and 1927 excited him hardly less than his pioneer work in Britain; eager to preserve contact with his indigenous roots, he made trips to Australia and New Zealand in 1924 and

1926. The second trip was a concert tour, though recitalizing gradually became less important for him not only than composing, but also than teaching. He became an instructor in piano at Chicago College of Music between 1928 and 1931, and for the year of 1932–3 accepted an appointment as Head of Music at New York University's College of Fine Arts, though he had previously declined several similar offers on the grounds that he was a non- or anti-academic. Among his pupils in New York were appropriately numbered Bernard Herrmann, most intelligent of film composers, and Morton Gould, an inventive composer of 'light' music, albeit without Percy's renovative qualities.

Grainger's later American years were increasingly geared to an educational context. He had long dabbled in what we now call World Music; in the thirties and forties this interest grew obsessive. Grainger's ethnomusicological work mattered not so much because he unearthed little- or unknown areas of music, as because of the startling acuity of the parallels he discovered between disparate phenomena: such as the music of the improvising polyphonists he heard in Polynesia, and the music of the then almost-unknown Perotin, twelfth-century *maître de chapelle* at Notre Dame (to which he'd been introduced by the priest-scholar, Dom Anselm Hughes). The prophetic implications of Grainger's intelligence strike home when we note that an affinity such as Percy here observes proves to be a cornerstone of Steve Reich's Process Music thirty or more years later. Reich visited exotic terrains in pursuit of his musical ideals; Grainger, fired by practical experience in a foreign field, was led by it into research. Complementarily, it is no less typical that he should have outraged an audience of composition students during his year at New York University by declaring that the three greatest composers ever were Bach, Delius, and Duke Ellington: Bach for his faith-affirming pulse, the consistency of his figuration, and the glorious lucidity of his counterpoint; Delius for his proud independence, his concern with elementals, and his harmonically audacious subjectivity; and Ellington for his mating of urban immediacy, and even the world of commerce, with (in Allen Ginsberg's words) 'the beauty of his wild forebears, a mythology he cannot inherit— nostalgias of another life' that might, vicariously, be also ours.

If Grainger spurned European notions like sonata and symphony—he was less dismissive of fugue which he thought not a form but a principle with democratic implications—this was

8

because he had no ambitions in that direction. He was fired by a more urgent need: to reanimate, by making and doing, an effete civilization that, in its excessive concern with sensibility, had forfeited common sense and animal virility. The exploitations and corruptions of mercantile industrialism were, in his view, only the last and grubbiest nail in civilization's coffin. His notions may have been naive, for when once a Shakespeare and a Beethoven have been evolved or invented, one cannot pretend they never happened. Even so, he reminded us of truths we had forgotten, to our cost; it is not surprising that today his music and writings strike chords to which people, especially young people, gratefully respond.

In his last years Grainger's excitement about bringing 'All the World's Music to All the World' was balanced by more hermetic pursuits, for in his studio at White Plains he became increasingly preoccupied with his concept of Free Music, in furtherance of which he developed, with the assistance of a physicist, Burnett Cross, a number of weird mechanical devices. These were an attempt to hit back at the very world which machines had manufactured rather than created: for the Free Music Machines, designed to encompass an infinite gradation of pitches, took up the preoccupations of his earliest original compositions, especially the *Hill Songs* which had sought for the music of Nature Herself. That wild ambition had in turn been fostered by childhood experience when, listening to running water, the boy Percy had realized that the sonic possibilities inherent in Nature had been barely tapped in conventional music. He hoped that Nature's elemental sounds—turning earth, whistling wind, sizzling fire, and gurgling water—might create an audible universe whereby he could communicate with people directly, without intermediaries such as notation and humanly operated instruments. An ultimate twist to the paradox is that although electrophonics made the realization of Grainger's ideas feasible, he distrusted their antihuman mechanization. Again, he wanted it both ways, cultivating selfhood and selflessness simultaneously: so that the machines found their way to the Grainger Museum in Melbourne—the temple he built (mostly on the considerable earnings of his pop numbers and the residue of his career as a virtuoso) 'as a kind of artistic life insurance against my coming death. Let there be no records wanting, of any folk, language, song history, not even of myself: perhaps least of all of myself.' There the machines squat mutely, a melancholy memorial to an extraordinary man.

Above all, a paradoxical man: who was at once an avant-garde experimentalist ahead of his time, and a pop composer dedicated to the continuity of tradition and of the common touch. Those aims were not, as he affected to believe, antithetical, but complementary: his lollipops were most frequently performed on, and often designed for, a mechanical contrivance (falsely) tuned in equal temperament; whereas his Free Music Machines, encompassing an infinite gradation of pitches, could emulate the flexible tuning and volatile intonation of unaccompanied folk-singers. Paradox typified his temperament, no less than his musical activities. Like his hero Delius, he could be a lonely misogynist and lover of solitudinous mountain peaks, while also being a gregarious socialite who was married, in the Hollywood Bowl before an audience variously estimated at 15,000 and 23,000 people, to his Nordic princess, celebrated in a gaudy gala performance of a Bridal Song especially composed for the occasion. If Percy's attempt to 'free' music proved abortive, and if his original compositions amount to less than he thought or hoped, one may at least say that both his composition and his pianism offered release from moribund routine, and some hope of artistic fulfilment not merely for an élite, but for all sorts and conditions of men and women. His personality and his music make for life: which is a composer's first obligation, especially in a society too addicted, as is ours, to greed and death.

Grainger's empiricism means that he is a difficult composer to 'study', if not to enjoy. His bibliography, given the hair-raising confusion of the many versions he made of works veering between composition, arrangement, and transcription, resists categorization: the more so because he often presented his works in 'elastic' scorings—a habit attributable to his pragmatic approach and perhaps to his early experience with music-hall and theatre orchestras. But although this makes matters difficult for librarians, it is not of major significance for those who enjoy Percy's music. Categorization is not synonymous with wisdom, especially in reference to a creature as mercurial as Percy Grainger. What matters is that the current spate of new recordings of his music, and the wider dissemination of his however-disorderly writings, suggest that his therapeutic value to our beleaguered times is increasingly recognized. This book, written thirty years after his death from cancer at White Plains Hospital, is a modest enquiry into how his therapy works.

# I
# PERCY PUCK AND PETER PAN
*'rippingly boyish'*

Percy Grainger was an infant prodigy; certainly his mother thought he was. To delve into the depths of the Grainger psyche is not the aim of this book, which is about his music. Even so, the weird story of Grainger's life is inseparable from his art; and only when we have read John Bird's account of his early days do we begin to understand why boyhood was and remained the heart of his creation. A child of exceptional physical beauty, with a doting mother and largely absent father, Percy battened on his dreams and fancies and, endowed by God and his parents with unusual abilities as a pianist, found himself, in his early teens, siphoning those fancies into keyboard music.

Admittedly, these small piano pieces, all written 'for Mother', are not strikingly fanciful, let alone memorable, for their idiom is that of the nineteenth-century salon music that graced suburban Australian parlours. Several of the pieces are simply called, in German, *Klavierstück*, and are in a style a long way after the slighter piano pieces of Schumann and Brahms. Mostly in ternary form, they sound like a spontaneous overflow from Schumann's *Album for the Young*; and there is point in the fact that Percy's trigger to creation should have been a composer himself powerfully affected by childhood experience. Grainger's boyhood pieces lack the magic of Schumann's genius, though they intermittently irradiate cliché with waywardness. A typical instance is the little 'Andante con moto', probably written when Percy was 15, a piece differing from childish Schumann only in being more open-eared and wider-eyed, since the weight of German tradition is not directly behind it. More touching, and more personal, is *Peace*, which moves in gently homophonic diatonic concords, but sounds more lonesome than peaceful because the rhythms are curiously irresolute. A livelier piece, oddly but characteristically called 'Saxon Twiplay', has a comparably directionless effect, perhaps because its 'plaited' technique leads to metrical ambiguity. The title is an early indication of Grainger's lifelong obsession with

Nordic culture—strong enough to encourage him to dismiss conventional Italian musical terminology in favour of 'blue-eyed English'. Associating the toughly Nordic with Australia, a rough new land, Grainger insisted that all these early pieces were, in their empiricism, essentially Australian, though no manifestation of Australianism is specific. At the time Grainger had no knowledge of or interest in genuine Aborigine music, and white Melbourne parlour music was European rather than indigenous. Grainger's Australian qualities lay rather in his innocence, observable not only in these brief parlour pieces, but also in his first attempts at more substantial, or at least longer, composition.

When he was 16 Percy composed what he appropriately called *A Youthful Suite* for theatre orchestra—the theatre orchestra being, of course, the only medium for concerted music he had contact with in his native city. Two movements have some interest, not because they are good music, but because they are harbingers of things to come. 'Rustic Dance' is closer to pretend-rural music in Edwardian musical comedy than to a genuine folk dance such as will occupy Grainger's attention in later life; but it has occasional hints of modality and a typical bumpkin charm, while its second tune, with oompah accompaniment, has a rudimentarily Elgarian flow. 'Eastern Intermezzo', on the other hand, reflects the boy Grainger's excursions into Melbourne's Chinatown, being 'Chinky' Edwardian theatre music, with xylophone-like repeated notes, rather than the real thing. His 'Chu-Chin-Chow' was a game like his 'Merrie Englande', though both meant more than similar games played by youths who never developed an obsessional interest in World Music. One shouldn't read too much into these pieces, but can say that they are remarkably assured for a young man with minimal musical experience. Their confidence springs from their composer's exceptionally acute ear.

In the following year, 1899, Grainger wrote an *English Waltz* for theatre orchestra, later dished up for solo piano, and for two pianos, four hands. Pre-dating Percy's obsession with folk-song, it is again 'English' in evoking Edwardian parlour and music-hall, which Grainger must have revelled in immediately after his arrival in England, no doubt because such music reminded him of the Melbourne parlours he had left behind. Most effective in its solo-piano version, which Percy frequently featured in his recitals, the *English Waltz* cunningly exploits the cross (hemiola) rhythms typical of the nineteenth-century dance, though the fun is ribald rather than sophisticated. In the same year Grainger worked on a more considerable piece which he called *English Dance*, ambitiously intended for large orchestra with organ, but empirically adapted in 'elastic scoring' for two pianos, six hands, and for various divisions of the large orchestra, culminating in a 'room-music' version for piano four hands, harmonium, solovox, organ, and 'four or five' strings. Again the piece is English not in being folky, but in evoking demotic English life in the arbitrary form of an unbroken, impetuous-rhythmed action-piece lasting not far off nine minutes. It lives up to Percy's breathless description of it to Roger Quilter: 'some hint of allround boyish throb or buoyant boyish limber elastic meddlesomeness of the English breed. ENGLAND DANCING, omnibuses racing one way, football rushes, newsboys' cunning cycling, factories clanging and booming away, fast trains shuddering past, fire-horses—general reliable rolicing [*sic*] riot and disciplined disorder.' The effect of the freely rambling unstoppable music is very like that of Percy's prose, agog with demotic vitality but stuttering in over-exuberance. In his note Grainger refers to the 'athletic energy and rich warmth' of tunes like 'Come lasses and lads', which he hopes he is emulating. Perhaps coincidentally rather than by intention, the *Dance* begins in A major, traditionally a key of blue-eyed youth and hope. But it doesn't stay there since, after a ripely gooey passage of chromatic sequences, it modulates to the subdominant for the Tune. The effect is similar to the trio section of a Sousa march, which is always in the subdominant and always more lyrically sustained than the march proper, making us 'feel good' in both senses of the phrase. If we think of the first march-section in military terms, the trio-chorus is 'What We Are Fighting For, Hearth and Home'; if the march is not military but belongs to college or club, the trio takes us from a general awareness of community to communion with Toms, Dicks, and Harrys for whom we have particular affection. The piece may end, still in the *sub*dominant but very loud, because it tells us that these individual Toms and Harrys, Janes and Joans, *are* the Nation—Percy's 'English breed'. The gregarious friendliness of the *English Dance* sums up what Percy, at least in early youth, meant by democracy.

But if the *English Waltz* and *English Dance* were native, even provincial, works, Grainger also produced in 1899 a substantial piece with no overt local associations. His *Love Verses from the*

*Song of Solomon* were elastically scored for mezzo-soprano and tenor solos, mixed chorus, accompanied by a chamber orchestra of 'twelve or more instruments, or by harmonium (single or massed) or pipe organ, piano duet, and any of the instruments of the Chamber Orchestra'. The work was a hangover from his student days rather than music springing from the life he was immediately living: as may be implicit in the fact that the words are from the Authorized Version of the Bible, a book of which Percy young or old did not approve, although, being from the Song of Solomon, they display eroticism, to which Percy had no objection. Although the work did not make Grainger's reputation and didn't deserve to, its techniques are prophetically of some interest. Melodically, the lines are flexible and modal; both in their often pentatonic contours and in their volatile speech-rhythms (entailing frequent changes of time-signature), they hint at the contours of English folk-song, though the work was composed before Grainger's conscious 'conversion'. The virtues of the piece lie in its sinuous polyphony and in the tonal freedom that goes with it. The opening section seems to be in the Aeolian mode on G, with an ambivalent sixth now major, now minor. This sidles into a similarly ambivalent mode on F sharp, then up to A flat, which may be enharmonically identical with G sharp. But this freedom doesn't altogether convince, being directionless rather than liberating; the chromatic harmony generated by the tonal flexibility fails to add bite and intensity, so that when the coda returns to the themes of the opening section, now a tone lower in F, the effect is indeterminate rather than assuaging.

Perhaps in reaction to the *Song of Solomon*'s somewhat anodyne eroticism and exoticism, Grainger cast his next work in homelier vein. Indeed it was directly a consequence of friendship, being written in 1901 for Herman Sandby, a Frankfurt Conservatory buddy, and himself to play on a duo cello-and-piano tour. He boyishly called it *A Lot of Rot*, but changed the title to the more serviceable (if hardly less 'rippingly' boyish) *Youthful Rapture* when he made an orchestral version of the piano part. In the new form the piece was premiered by Beatrice Harrison of nightingale fame, under Malcolm Sargent, but immediately disappeared from the repertory. This is a slight pity for the piece, although no masterwork, is the first Grainger music to suggest, in its self-communing, early Delius—and this before the two men had met.

Much of Delius's music was a search for a vanished Eden, usually associated with childhood; Grainger managed to live in some such Eden for much of his adult life. It is interesting that although we tend to think of Delius's pastoralism as English, his boyhood Eden often had an American rather than British ambiance: as is evident in his choral and orchestral work *Appalachia*, based on an 'old slave song', and still more in his setting of Whitman's *Sea Drift*. Similarly, Grainger's early excitement over boyhood heroism in his Nordic sagas had an American overspill. In a letter written in 1907 to his Danish lover Karen Holten, he pays touching tribute to Mark Twain's Tom Sawyer and Huck Finn, remarking that,

if ever you come to Australia or America, I'm sure you'll see what a rippingly true picture of the wildly happy and heroically self-centred boylife of the New World the Tom Sawyer–Huck Finn tales are; nature makes a real personal appeal to one because one really meets it alone; and neither it nor oneself are much shackled, and life isn't so heavy and serious that it sheds a bloody blighting shadow even over childhood. When I've made my money, I'll be a kid again; my mind won't be old and I'll go for Iceland and West Ireland and Scottish Highlands and Norwegian Highlands and south Africa and Australian bush country, like a baby.

Grainger not only realized these geographical ambitions; he remained a Peter Pan whose true creativity was achieved, on his own admission, between the ages of 15 and 25, though over many years he 'worked over' his original inspirations, dishing them up in sundry forms for various media. The collocation, in his comments on Mark Twain, between childish chumminess and the lonesomeness involved in meeting Nature 'unshackled', is to become a leitmotiv throughout his creative life. He was already simultaneously a Lonely Desert Man and a member of the Happy Tribes—anticipatorily to refer to a minor work of deep autobiographical significance, to which in later chapters we'll be devoting an amount of attention disproportionate to its musical merit.

Two literary influences, apart from his generalized delight in heroic sagas, dominate Grainger's early youth, one being American, the other English. There is no cause for surprise in the fact that Percy should have been bowled over by the omnivorously demotic *Song of Myself* of that great American prophet of free enterprise, Walt Whitman—the more so, perhaps, because it entailed an element of sexual ambivalence. Given his paradoxical nature, Percy rejoiced in inconsistency and didn't notice, or didn't care, that he, whose life-work was to be focused on a recovery of the folk-past, should have found a clarion-call in Whitman's wholesale rejection of history. Although the New World may have 'received with joy' the legacies of European feudalism, Whitman yet doubted whether 'of the great poems received from abroad and from the ages, and today enveloping and penetrating America, there is one that is consistent with these United States, or essentially applicable to them as they are or are to be. Is there one whose underlying basis is not a denial and insult to Democracy?' 'NO, there is not', Percy retorted, adding that the remark was applicable to Australia no less than to America: so that it must be his 'joyous duty' to play his part in 'the creation of music that should reflect the easy-going, happy-go-lucky yet robust hopefulness and the undisciplined individualistic energy of the athletic out-of-doors Anglo-Saxon newer nations'. He decided to give this form and body when, in Paris in 1900, at the dawn of a new century, he gazed raptly at a statue of George Washington. He would compose an act of homage to Whitman in the shape of a *Marching Song of Democracy*—music of 'comradely athletic affectionate humanity chanting the great pride of man in himself; the underlying urges to be heroic but not martial, exuberant but not provocative, passionate but not dramatic, athletic but not competitive'. He wrote the work during the summer of 1901, in Frankfurt in the wake of his student days. In it the 19-year-old youth rejected 'Europe', not yet realizing how much the age-old traditions of 'Unwritten Music' were to mean to him. He literally carried his piece out of Europe, revising it in 1908 in Australia, where he thought it belonged, and finally scoring it in 1915–16, in New York, which had then become his democratically rootless, global-village Home from Home. Even so, blood ran thicker than water; he dedicated the work 'to my darling Mother, united with her in loving admiration of Walt Whitman'.

Whitman's aboriginality, in his great poems and especially in *A Song of Myself*, is childlike only in the sense that he was concerned with beginnings and discoveries, some of which had far-reaching, even frightening consequences. But Grainger's *Marching Song of Democracy* is simply childish, with the vernal charm of its innocence but with no sturdier substance. A piece for big kids, it was originally intended for the whistling voices of men, women, and children. No instruments were called for beyond those

Nature endowed people with, though the work ended up scored for full orchestra, with batteries of extra percussion. Bells, marimba, electric glockenspiel and xylophone, piano, bar-piano, harmonium, and organ riotously contribute to the hubbub, while the voices are intermittently asked to emulate drums, trumpets, and other festive instruments. At least the music lives up to the composer's description of it, quoted in the previous paragraph; it is heroic, exuberant, passionate, and athletic, though it may not always evade competitiveness, provocation, and the martial. The tunes and harmony are basically plain diatonic; the rhythms swagger, enhancing exuberance with syncopation and the overriding of bar-lines. The vocal lines incorporate a fair measure of free polyphony and of counterpoint: of which, as we have noted, Percy approved as manifestations of democratic principle. A rich resonance, strictly speaking 'vulgar' in something like Charles Ives's early hymnic vein, is generated, while the free rhythms and volatile modulations suggest optimism untrammelled, striding into an unknown but desirable future. That democratic men and women, along with their children, march in togetherness is manifest in the fact that through all the metrical time-shifts the crotchet pulse remains constant. Tramping feet are at one, even as the voices modulate widely and wildly, incrementally reinforced by the real instruments whose sounds they onomatopoeically imitate. A tremendous racket is unleashed, attaining climax when the choir sways in parallel triads in contrary motion, while the keyed percussion rise to frenzy over a cavernous organ pedal note, preferably played on a Mighty Wurlitzer. The cavorting modulations finally reach F sharp major, with everyone in full pelt. This is one of the earliest instances of Grainger's use of six-sharped F sharp major in association with states of rapture or ecstasy or, as here, with communal orgy, rather than with mystical transcendence. Indeed Grainger's F sharp major is never mystical in a religious sense although—as we'll see later—it may be connected with 'sacred' emotions of ineffable tenderness, usually in reference to his mother.

If the climactic end of *Marching Song of Democracy* might superficially be called Ivesian, the comparison should not be pushed far: for Ives's 'naivety' is never merely that, whereas Percy's naivety is here indeed kids' stuff, 'rippingly' boyish, moving forward maybe, but to no discernible end. Yet the open-ended feeling, if a limitation, is also a strength. If Grainger has not here created great or even very good music, he has uncompromisingly saluted youth and potential green pastures. In this sense the provisional nature of the piece—whether in the full version or in versions for wind-band, organ, and/or massed pianos—is part of its 'philosophy'. The other literacy obsession of Grainger's adolescence both supports and (again paradoxically) counteracts Whitman's aboriginal freedom, for Grainger worshipped Rudyard Kipling both as an imperialistic Nietzschean superman and as a swashbuckling Boys' Own hero who was not only a kind of British Huck Finn, but at heart a Child of Nature, like Mowgli of the *Jungle Books*. We should not forget that the finest flower of Kipling's genius may be in his stories and verses for children— who are addressed at a fairly early age in the marvellous *Just So Stories*, the techniques of which have analogies with the repetitive and incantatory devices of fairy-tales and sagas; at a more mature age in the mythic remakings of English history in *Puck of Pook's Hill* and *Rewards and Fairies*; and most of all in the *Jungle Books* and *Kim*, those legendary evocations of boyhood experience in a physically and metaphysically remote India. Most of these stories are rites of passage and myths of rebirth, and one suspects that Grainger half-identified with Mowgli, the half-caste boy nurtured by forest beasts, away from civilization, in the jungle's depths.

Grainger made more than fifty settings of Kipling's verse, most though not all of which date from the late nineties and from the first decade of the twentieth century. As usual, they were rehashed over many years in different versions, and Grainger had no doubt that his *Jungle Book* settings were the most characteristic and significant of his early works, apart from the *Hill Songs*. He tells us that in them,

above all in 'The Beaches of Lukkanon', I developed my mature harmonic style—that is to say, harmony in unresolved discords. To the best of my knowledge, such a procedure was unknown at that time and must be considered an Australian contribution to musical progress. So through the [parcel of Kipling] books my father sent me in 1897, I became what I have remained ever since, a composer whose musical output was based on patriotism and racial consciousness.

The Australianism of this patriotism and racial consciousness would seem in these pieces to be latent rather than patent, and Percy was a trifle self-indulgent in his claims for the 'aboriginality' of his free dissonances. He was on the mark, however, in describing the eleven 'Jungle' pieces he finally published as a suite, as 'my Jungle Book cycle, begun in 1898 and finished in 1947, and composed as a protest against civilization'. The suite was, of course, 'dedicated to my beloved Mother'.

Although called a cycle by the composer, the eleven published songs are scored for various combinations of voices and instruments. The text of the song placed first, 'The Fall of the Stone' (1901–4) doesn't even come from the *Jungle Books* but from *Plain Tales from the Hills*, also a product of Kipling's Indian years. The scoring is for mixed chorus, with two violas, three cellos, one double bass, two horns or alto saxophones, and two bassoons or baritone saxophones. Cor anglais, euphonium, harmonium, and piano may be added at will, and all the instrumental parts may be doubled or tripled according to the size of the chorus. There is little evidence here of the harmonic licentiousness that Grainger refers to and perhaps boasts of; but one may grant that this beast-song displays an 'Australian' empiricism in its rousing 6/8 tune, with recurrent metrical displacements (bars of 2/4 or 1/4), perhaps reflecting the immediacy of shanty-town pub performance. The *ad hoc* instrumentation reinforces this, and Grainger's scoring is habitually not that of premeditated concert performance, but of some potential music-making ritual, whether of work or of play.

More musically substantial is the second number, written in 1905, this time simply for mixed chorus unaccompanied. It is a strophic song, beginning in D major though often with modally flattened seventh, and typified by its hypnotically syncopated rhythm. The harmonic texture, sometimes dividing into six, seven, or eight parts, is rich but not cloying, for the swinging rhythm, corporeally portraying the surge of life at the instigation of the new day's sun, propels all before it. As in *Marching Song of Democracy*, we are swept forward by the unremittent rhythm, the progressively freer part-writing, and the ever-wilder key changes which—like Mowgli and the beasts through the Spring Running—are always moving foward to no goal except Nature's inevitable rebirth. This convinces, as *Marching Song of Democracy* doesn't, perhaps because Nature's new birth is indubitable, whereas democracy's onward march is an open question. Certainly we can take it when the song, having begun in D major-minor, unabashedly ends in C major, because that is where it finds itself. Unpredictability is of the essence: which is also why the tune, mostly moving stepwise in its padding rhythm, relishes suddenly outrageous leaps to high notes. This is potently jungloid, though the choral textures intermittently recall barber-shop homophony or even the Edwardian parlour. It matters that the Edwardian present is manifest to this degree; if it weren't, we might not realize how right Grainger was to describe these songs as 'a protest against civilization'.

The complementary 'Night Song in the Jungle' is also *a cappella*, but for men only. Although the pulse is 'easy-going' in a lilting 6/8, the song evokes the 'hour of pride and power', when the jungle is predatory. Prideful power is emphasized by Grainger's free dissonances, while the easy-goingness comes simply from hunting being a part of natural process. The piece, dating back to 1898, is brief, and nowhere near as interesting as the next number 'The Inuit', which, although from the *Second Jungle Book*, is about Eskimos in the frozen wastes. The theme—the corruption and spoliation of the noble savage by white traders—unsurprisingly provokes Grainger to music of peculiar force, and is scored for unaccompanied mixed chorus in C sharp major, with seven bristling sharps! Percy must have been deeply moved by the heroic theme thus to carry his tipsily 'high' tonality to its ultimate point, beyond his favoured F sharp major. The haunting, mostly stepwise-moving tune is treated homophonically in six parts that may swell to seven or eight. Again, the free movement of the parts creates richly chromatic textures, surging through modulations not determined by convention. The end, asserting the Eskimos' proud independence 'beyond the white man's ken', is 'vehemently' in E flat major. If this sounds surprising in relation to the initial C sharp, it also sounds right, probably because it is 'really' D sharp major, two more stages up the cycle of fifths, and so double-sharped as to be unnotatable!

'The Beaches of Lukkanon', begun in the 'Kipling year' of 1898, was not 'finished off' until 1941, when it was offered as a birthday present to his then-dead mother. Although the words are from the *Second Jungle Book*, they are again about that other wilderness, the frozen North, and the heroic victims are here not people but seals. This makes for a very 'green', if whitely icy, piece, scored for mixed chorus with 'nine or more' strings and harmonium. Grainger thought this song the pearl of the set and it is indeed, prompted by the incorruptible seals, noble. The first section, in the Aeolian mode on G, is in four parts in a flowing march rhythm, with stark parallel fifths appropriate to a primitive waste. The middle section in benedictory G major, changes the march pulse to 12/8, dotted crotchet equalling the previous crotchet. The choir is split into groups singing in antiphony, with dissonant clashes between parallel triads. As we may see from Example 1, the passage warrants, given its early date, the pat on the back Grainger gave himself for harmonic enterprise, especially since throughout the section strings and harmonium sustain chromatic chords as ostinatos. The presence of the harmonium really does make a difference to this passage. Percy's enthusiasm for the instrument sometimes carried him into hyperbole, even to the point of opining that, 'if I were forced to choose one instrument only for chamber music, I would choose the harmonium without hesitation, for it seems to me the most sensitive and intimately expressive of all instruments'. More soberly, he would seem to have regarded it as a modern continuo instrument more effective, because more audible, than the harpsichord, and invaluable in that its gluey effect could bind together Nature's disparities. There's an implicit allegory in bringing the harmonium, redolent of cosy parlours, chapels, and pub snugs, into the wilds. The ecstatic idyll contrasts the paradisaical seal rookeries on the Aleutian Islands with the depradations wrought by the wicked sealers, who have the last word in a stern, brief da capo of the original lament.

'Red Dog', for unaccompanied men's voices, was composed, not merely rewritten, in 1941, as another birthday present for dead Rose. It's a beast-piece, chanted by hounds a-hunting, in an adventurous style depending partly on the chromaticism of its triple-rhythmed tune, partly on its metrical irregularities, incorporating half-beats. The onomatopoeic baying at the end can be blood-curdling—the more so because, without instrumental support, the piece is extremely difficult to sing.

'The Peora Hunt', dating from 1906, is about riding men and buffalo, tough creatures in a rough landscape. Conceived on a large scale, it is for mixed chorus basically in five parts but sometimes divided, with an instrumental accompaniment of harmonium and piano; or two bassoons or cellos and piano with or without harmonium; or strings and piano with or without harmonium; or one or two bassoons, strings and piano, with or without harmonium. Tonality is very free, centring on a modalized, pentatonic-tending G; the textures are often primitive, with bare parallel fifths and tangy false relations. The rhythms are again

Example 1  'The Beaches of Lukkanon', p. 3.

corporeal but irregular, imitating physical gestures in measures of 2½/4!

The next number is another hunting song, dating back to the Kipling year of 1898. 'The Hunting Song of the Seeone Pack' is powerful wolf-music scored for wolvish men in five parts, climactically expanded to seven. Kipling's metrically vigorous verses serve, as usual, to inspire a galloping tune in 12/8 hunting pulse, embracing an oddly chromatic refrain with Aeolian-flavoured diatonicism. The end—contrasting the clinging smoothness of the 'feet in the jungle that leave no mark', in swaying but dissonant

Example 1 *cont.*

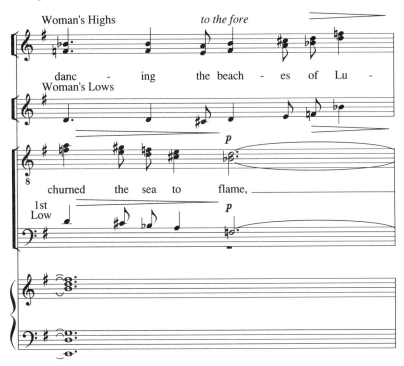

parallel thirds, with the ultimate hunting-holla—carries a tremendous punch. This is countered by the next number, 'Tiger, tiger', yet another hunting song for male voices, with tenor and baritone solos poised against choric refrains. But this song, dated 1905, turns out to be about the bitter aspect of hunting's end, namely dying. The final cadence, softly swelling to six voices, is especially moving in its grammatically unrelated concords.

The words of 'The Only Son', though taken form Kipling's *Many Inventions*, earn a place in the Jungle cycle because they tell a tale about a boy who wonders whether he was born of womankind or, like Mowgli, 'on a shaggy hide'. Written as late as 1945 and lavishly scored, the piece is not really different from the early cycle in style, though it is possibly still freer in rhythm and more angular in line: as is evident in the wide-flung opening invocation for soprano in Example 2. In addition to soprano and tenor solo and mixed chorus, the score calls for a band consisting

Example 1 *cont.*

Example 2 'The Only Son', opening, soprano line only.

minimally of harmonium, piano, two violins, viola, two cellos, and double bass. There are also parts for cor anglais, three clarinets, bass clarinet, two bassoons, two horns, three trombones, kettle-drums, and harp: which seems a lot to ask for a piece lasting three minutes. The point is presumably to encourage as many people as possible to join in, as occasion offers. Grainger's claims for the venturesomeness of his harmony are justified by this place, though in 1945 it is not as startling as it would have been in 1898. The song ends on an unresolved dissonance when the boy is reclaimed by the wild wolves, though we're not told what this means in respect to his future or lack of one.

The number placed last, written for Mother in 1905, is appro-priately the most crucial, for 'Mowgli's Song Against People' makes the attack on 'civilization' overt. As in natural process, death is necessary to create life, which can burgeon only when 'the trees are on you, the house-beams fall, and the bitter Karela shall cover you all'. The forceful words beget forceful music, flowing in triplets in a 3/4 pulse, and scored for mixed chorus with seven strings weighted to the bass, with the usual piano and harmonium and with optional oboes and cor anglais. Although less wild than the previous late-dated number, this 'Song against People' is no less remote from the Edwardian parlour. The free-dom of line, rhythm, and tonality is Ivesian, though at that date Grainger couldn't have known any of Ives's music. The modality, rooted on G, wanders weirdly but finally resolves, through a dec-orated plagal cadence in seven parts, on a protracted, pianissimo G major triad. The effect is regretful, even nostalgic, perhaps because the song, and indeed the cycle, asks a question: does this music celebrate a new birth, or a Fall from Eden? The answer, of course, is both.

Grainger's Kipling settings were, we've noted, mostly composed in the decade after 1897, the year in which his father sent him that parcel of Kipling books. The pieces were all revised, some of them several times, between the date of their conception and 1947, when the selected eleven numbers were published as a *Jungle Book* cycle. Grainger spoke of the set as one of his earliest major works, but the suite was never a 'work' in the conventional sense, but a collection of choric songs springing from *ad hoc* circumstances and scored for *ad hoc* forces. It would therefore be difficult to perform the cycle as a whole, and this has been done only once—at Aldeburgh in 1982. This is a pity, since the numbers make an impressive cumulative effect because all stem from the same impulse—the 'protest against civilization' and the celebration of Nature's new births so vividly enacted in Kipling's verses. Kipling not only gave Grainger his basic theme; he also suggested techniques apposite to it. Both his use of archaically hieratic language comparable with that of sagas and fairy-tales, and his rumbustiously corporeal, 'tribal' rhythms found a ready response in the young Australian. In Kipling's verse communal 'savagery' fuses with the jaunty virility of the Edwardian music-hall. Just such a synthesis of natural primitivism with the urbanly demotic is to typify Grainger's music, not merely in these pieces, but recurrently throughout his life.

An appendix to the *Jungle Book* series is the 'Zanzibar Boat Song', an instrumental piece inspired by verses from *Plain Tales from the Hills*, scored for six hands on one piano. The (unheard) words of the verses describe the burning of a corpse upon the sand, invoking the Spirit of Fire as a Light of Guidance to call home the 'plunging boats'. Spirits of fire and lights of guidance were just up Grainger's street, and he produces splendid 'action music', restricted to one hypnotic rowing rhythm and a few harmonic patterns that create a trance-like effect through reiteration. The scoring for six hands on one piano contributes powerfully to the music's density: which may be why Grainger uncharacteristically made no attempt to dish the piece up in other formats. The music is not, like the unsung words, fierce, but it is inexorable.

'Zanzibar Boat Song' was composed, contemporaneously with the *Jungle Book* settings, in 1902. Between 1902 and 1905 Grainger also made fine settings of verses from *Barrack Room Ballads* and *The Seven Seas*. For the vernacular primitivism of these Boer War soldiers' and sailors' songs Grainger invents a demotic style no less convincing than Kipling's verses. Especially impressive is 'The Sea Wife', from *The Seven Seas*, for to match Kipling's stirring marching-ballad Grainger lights on a no-less stirring tune, scored for mixed chorus accompanied by brass band or by strings, or by a mixture of both, or by piano duet. At first the tune is in the Dorian mode on F, but with ambiguous sixth; pentatonic formulae are pervasive in the modality. It's as easily memorable as a folksong without being one; such chromatic harmonies as are introduced in no way compromise the tune's momentum. Although the conception is basically strophic, it is also developmental, for the heroic tie between the sea wife and the greedy ocean impels the music through wide-ranging modulations—to a modal C sharp minor, a more or less diatonic D flat major, a chromaticized C major and, surprisingly but convincingly, to a climactic B flat major. Kipling's body rhythms, combined with his narrative zest, make for a popular verse that steers Grainger into an urban popular music with the authenticity of rural folk art. Folk-song, chapel-hymn, and music-hall ballad are interfused.

Fine as is 'The Sea Wife', the best-known and perhaps the best of Grainger's Kipling settings outside the *Jungle Book* cycle is 'Danny Deever', from *Barrack Room Ballads*: a grimly comic hanging-ballad in folk question-and-answer form, scored for a small male unison chorus (or baritone solo), with a large male choir to chant the refrains. The modality is basically Dorian on C, though much of the solo line is pentatonic; the pulse is that of a thrustful but sombre march. Chromatics point the modality to stress the words' grim ironies, especially in the refrains wherein We the People raucously assuage guilt in laughing at it. Occasional half-beats also underline verbal significances, without compromising the vigour and rigour of the refrains; for instance at Danny's moment of death (see Example 3). Grainger must have recognized that in this memorably vulgar pop song of 1903 he'd bitten off not more than he could chew, for chew it he does, but more than he'd bargained for. He later rehashed it for a vast band of piccolo, two flutes, three clarinets, bass clarinet, two bassoons, double bassoon, four saxophones, four horns, three trumpets, euphonium, tuba, kettle drum, side drum, bass drum, cymbals, and strings—all for a piece lasting just over three minutes! It's improbable that this full version has ever been heard, but it ought to be. Its effect would be visceral, half-way between music-hall and early Verdi.

Although 'Danny Deever' is the only one of Grainger's Kipling settings that is fairly frequently heard, others would repay exploration. 'The Ballad of Bolivar', dating from 1901, is in Grainger's special F sharp major, opening with a sweeping tune covering two octaves. Grainger's comments on the incomplete sketches are revealing. He calls for 'a large men's chorus, strong woodwind, brass, horns, riotous unison shouting, twenty banjos, quite drunken; to my mind a really good tune and orchestral accompaniment, very music-hally'. Though there is a score in the Grainger Archives, this must be one of many Grainger audacities the performance of which is unrealizable. This bears on the kind

Example 3  'Danny Deever', pp. 10–11.

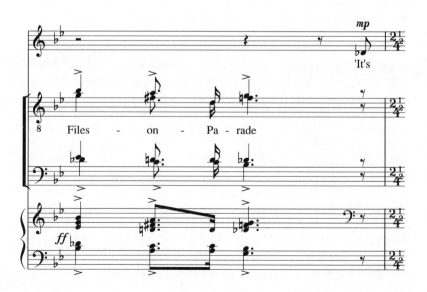

28

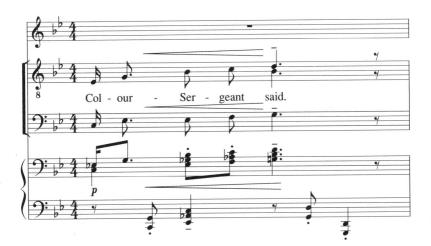

of composer Grainger is; and reminds us that we should not end this chapter without paying tribute to the herculean labours of Kay Dreyfus, one-time curator of the Grainger Museum, in charting the multiple versions of Grainger's Kipling settings, as they evolved over a period of more than forty years. In the nature of things she cannot establish 'definitive' versions. But Percy Grainger, like Charles Ives, did not admire completeness, and would have been gratified that Kay Dreyfus, telling us all there is to know, leaves us to take our pick.

## 2

# PERCY'S PARADOX

## *The Lonely Desert Man and the Hills Themselves*

Grainger's Kipling settings, created during the last years of the nineteenth century and the first decade of the twentieth, were not 'major' works, though he hoped that some of them might coalesce into one. And during those years he also worked on pieces conceived on a fairly large scale; in particular, he considered his *Hill Song No. 1* to be 'by far the best of all my compositions'. His note is worth quoting:

At the time of composing *Hill Song No. 1* (1901–2, aged 19–20) wildness and ferocity were the qualities in life and nature that I prized most and wished to express in music. In 1900 I had heard a very harsh-toned rustic oboe (*piffero*) in Italy, some extremely nasal double reeds at the Paris Exhibition, and bagpipes in the Scottish Highlands. I wished to weave these snarling sounds (which I had heard only in a single line melody) into a polyphonic texture as complex as Bach's, as democratic as Australia (by 'democratic' in a musical sense I mean a practice of music in which each voice that makes up the harmonic weft enjoys equal importance and independence as contrasted with 'undemocratic' music consisting of a dominating melody supported by subservient harmony). In this way I wished to give vent to feelings aroused by the soul-shaking hill-scapes I had recently seen on a three-day tramp in Western Argyllshire. I was not in favour of programme music. I had no wish to portray tonally any actual scene or even to record musically my impressions of nature. What I wanted to convey in my Hill Song was *the nature of the hills themselves*, as if the hills themselves were telling of themselves through my music, rather than that I, an onlooker, were recording my 'impressions' of the hills.

Grainger's *Hill Song* was thus his most radical attempt to create music totally aboriginal, independent of *a priori* rules and regulations. This music comes out as basically tonal because tonality is an acoustical fact of nature; but the lines are not restricted to any one 'natural' mode, tempered tonality, or preordained shape;

amorphously chromatic and polymodal, they are also so flexible in rhythm as to be barely notatable. That Grainger tried to notate them, changing the time signature almost every bar and indulging in half as well as whole beats, seems alien to the music's improvisatory spirit, and offers nearly insoluble difficulties for conductors. He was, however, facing up to problems inherent in any 'Unwritten Music', and anticipating his own later attempts precisely to re-produce the spontaneity of folk musics, including the Highland pipes that were among the triggers to this work. When it was performed in its original wind-band scoring Grainger encouraged the orchestral wind players—without, one imagines, conspicuous success—to revel in a nasally raucous tone and to allow their intertwining strands of melody to flow of their own volition, without scrupulous regard for ensemble. One may admire Grainger's predilection for gapped or 'wide-toned' folk scales as revealed in Example 4; still more may one wonder at the elasticity of rhythm, the variety of metre, and the independence of the woodwind scoring of the opening page of *Hill Song No. 1* (see Example 5). Even so, it is clear that this musically democratic freedom involves once more a paradox, and a semantic confusion: for the overflow of personal feeling is equated with subservience to the im-personality of Nature: Grainger's claim to have made a 'music of the hills themselves' can be no more than a metaphor, for hills do not speak our language, or any. He must have meant that he hoped to be a seismograph to Nature's murmurings, as did a composer of another New World, Charles Ives, in pieces such as *Central Park in the Dark* and *The Housatonic at Stockbridge*. Ives, however, leaves us in no doubt that although man and Nature coexist, they are not identical. Whether nature seems benign or minatory, she is always other than us; it is we who are 'aware' of her.

Grainger might have learned this not only from Ives, but also from the composer whom (with one exception to be discussed later) he admired above all others, Frederick Delius. Although a valedictory artist of Europe's twilight, Delius was also inspired— above all in *Sea-Drift*, arguably his most perfectly realized work— by the New World's Walt Whitman; and created, more than a decade later than Grainger's *Hill Song*, his own choral and orchestral *Song of the High Hills*. Questioned by Grainger, Delius bluntly retorted that in his piece he was *not* concerned with the hills themselves, but with the effect of their solitary spaces on a

Example 4 *Hill Song No. 1*, sketches, in Grainger's calligraphy

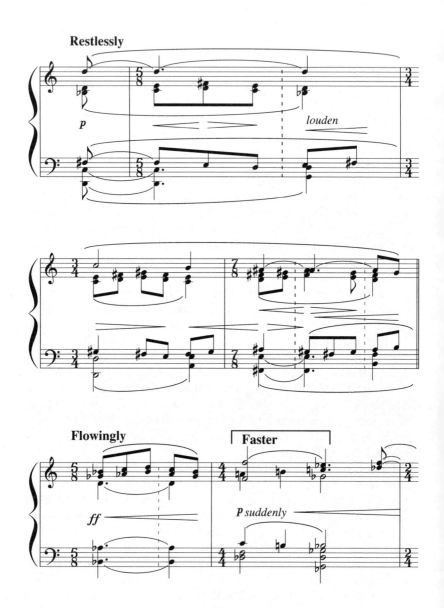

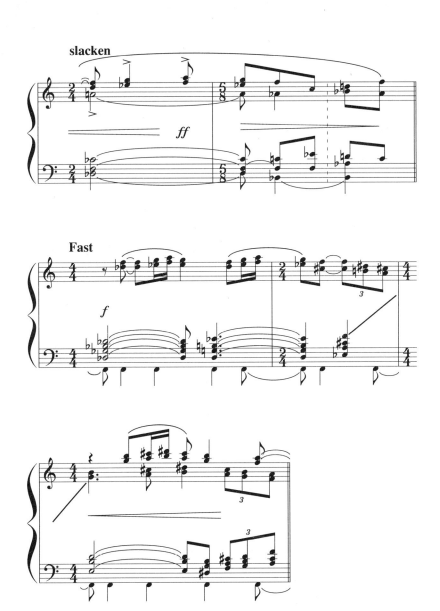

human being, himself. Although Delius rejected his native Bradford and modern industrial society, he was still a European, with (Wagnerian) standards of reference. But Grainger, making his hill song *ab ovo*, needed to be even more 'inspired' than was Delius, if his empiricism were to convince. He wasn't, and it doesn't; his hill songs are not great music, as is Delius's work. Even so, the audacity of the *Hill Song* may still make an impact, if it is convincedly performed in the freely interlaced textures and wild sonorities of the original wind-band version. Busoni, a proudly independent and rigorously intellectual musician who must have detested the *Hill Song*'s implicit 'philosophy', accorded the work grudging admiration, even though he heard it not in its wild-wind-dominated orchestration, but played, no doubt wildly, by the composer on piano.

The original version of *Hill Song No. 1* was scored in 1902, for two piccolos, six oboes, six cor anglais, six bassoons, and one double bassoon. *Hill Song No. 2*, appended in 1907, is not a new work but

Example 5   *Hill Song No. 1*, opening: orchestral score, in Grainger's calligraphy.

35

'a presentation of the fast, energetic elements of *Hill Song No. 1* as a single type whole, without contrasting elements of a slower, more dreamy nature'. The 'energetic' bits were somewhat extended, and the piece was scored for twenty-four wind instruments, and also dished up for two pianos. In 1923 both pieces were re-scored for symphony orchestra without violins, trombones, and tuba. The full orchestral versions iron out some of the metrical complexities, and so may be in performance more 'effective' if less authentic. But in any of the versions we can see why Grainger thought his *Hill Songs* ought to be 'by far' his best music, and also why they couldn't be, and weren't. Percy's faith in his *Hill Songs* is touchingly attested by the fact that he wove into their free textures a recurrent triplet phrase from his 1901 setting of Kipling's 'Mother o' Mine'.

Two other works among Grainger's 'originals' call for attention, both dating from a decade later. *The Warriors*, described as 'music for an imaginary ballet', was precipitated from a suggestion of Sir Thomas Beecham that Grainger should write a ballet for which he, Beecham, would provide a scenario. This was in the glamorous days of Diaghilev's Russian Ballet, and Grainger enthusiastically went ahead with the project during the very years (1913–16) when Stravinsky was gestating his *Rite of Spring*. Beecham produced no scenario, but Grainger's 'imaginary' one envisaged 'a sort of Valhalla gathering of childishly overbearing and arrogant savage men and women of all ages, arm in arm in united show of gay and innocent pride and animal spirits, fierce and exultant'. Grainger liked to pretend that this Global Village fiesta was a complement to Stravinsky's evocation of a sacrificial murder and fertility rite that, set in prehistoric Russia, fused destruction and re-creation, foreshadowing the 'death of Europe' in the World Wars. In fact, Grainger's eighteen-minute piece has nothing in common with Stravinsky's truly subversive masterwork, except that it is scored for a huge orchestra. Stravinsky's *Rite* still sends shivers down the spine, three-quarters of a century after the event. Grainger's *Warriors* never made anyone shiver, being rippingly boyish, like Percy himself; nor do they offer any audible evidence of the 'horror and hatred of war' that some commentators, perhaps animated by casual remarks of Grainger in old age, claim to hear in the piece. A more valid comparison is with Ives's boyhood evocations in pieces like *Three Places in New England*; and Grainger's techniques have affinities with Ives's in being—at the furthest pole from Stravinsky's meticulous precision—to a degree fortuitous. Inner parts come and go as whim dictates; batteries of percussion improvise with abandon; three pianos and an off-stage brass band, directed if need be by as many as three conductors, contribute to the hubbub. Though all this sounds Ivesian, the analogy is superficial. Ives's music discovers adult potential within childhood's empiricism, and links the fiesta experienced, in the first of the *Three Places*, through a boy's eyes and ears to the heartfelt retrospection of the third *Place*, which deals with memories of the composer's marriage and enduring love. Comparatively, Grainger's 'old Greek Heroes, shining black Zulus, flaxen-haired Vikings, lithe bright Amazons, squat Greenland women, Red Indians, negrito Fijans, and graceful cannibal Polynesians' are effervescent but callow. Un-differentiated from one another, they pass kaleidoscopically in glorious technicolour, with the eupepticism of a Sousa march and the streamlined high-jinks of American show-music. The structure is not symphonic but episodic, mirroring the passage of the colourful personnel. Prophetically, the piece has the effect of an audible comic strip and, as such, works excitingly—especially in the version for six hands on two pianos, in which the overlapping textures sparkle without becoming clotted.

Today, Grainger could have been a dazzlingly effective mediaman; and we may detect comic-strip elements in three of the four movements of his other main original work, the suite *In a Nutshell*. The title may refer to the work's encapsulation of the contrarious strands that had contributed to Grainger's music. Certainly the piece is non-symphonic, being a rag-bag garnered together over a number of years. The first piece, 'Arrival Platform Humlet', exists in versions for solo piano, two pianos, solo viola or 'massed violas', and for piano and theatre orchestra, variously put together between 1908 and 1916. The second piece, 'Gay but Wistful', was 'composed in 1912, worked out and scored 1915–16', in three versions for piano solo, two pianos, and piano with theatre orchestra. The third movement, 'Pastoral', is odd man out, deriving from the nature-music of the *Hill Songs* while being perhaps Grainger's most 'subjective' piece; it too exists in the same three versions, all dated 1916. The final 'Gumsuckers' March' was begun as early as 1905, but was dished up in the three versions in 1914. A fourth arrangement, for wind-band, was made late in Grainger's American years, in 1942.

'Arrival Platform Humlet' is a very odd piece that only Grainger could have thought up. The title means that it's a tune to be happily hummed to oneself while waiting at a railway station to meet friend or lover, an anticipatory oneness being suggested by the fact that it is consistently in unisons or octaves or, briefly, in parallel fifths (organum). The piece has no predetermined structure, being 'functional' as a hum ought to be; various snippets of tune are strung together as they occur to the hummer, with little repetition; Grainger gives a preview in Example 6. As is apparent, the tunes are quirkily rhythmed and volatilely modal, with unpredictable Lydian fourths and flat sixths and with no definitive keynote. This gives the music a genuine East-West, global-village flavour; we might be in Melbourne, Sydney, Tokyo, Hong Kong, San Francisco's Chinatown, New York's polyglot Greenwich Village, or London's Soho. This cosmopolitanism may be related to the fact that this was one of the first works Grainger composed after settling in New York, his global home from home. Although he was no longer adolescent, a New World youthfulness pervades the modal ambiguities and rhythmic dislocations: which would sound freshly invigorating on the 'humming' massed violas that Percy recommends. In complement, the second movement, 'Gay but Wistful', recalls the London years he'd left behind, being a distillation of the Edwardian music-hall that had afforded Percy such delight. The fetching tune really is 'gay but wistful', sounding simultaneously Cockney, suburban Australian, and raggily American.

The slow movement is remote from this urban cosiness. Lasting nine minutes, it is as 'serious' a piece as Grainger ever created; and he tinkered with it over a span of nine years. That it is called 'Pastoral' relates it to the *Hill Songs* but not to dreamy English nostalgia; for although it begins as a 12/8 monody in the Dorian mode on F, and flows into Delian pastoral chromatics, it is soon subjected to spasmodic polymodal and polymetrical metamorphoses, losing any defined tonal centre, and exploding in wild arabesques in contrarious rhythms. Superbly laid out on the keyboard, the music reveals ecstatic heights and neurasthenic depths more extreme than those of the *Hill Songs*—including, one suspects, the sexual desperation that Grainger banished from his public image. The later sections float into a glassy, Busoni-like bi- or polytonality, until the music fades out, 'beyond the horizon', in reverberating gong-strokes delivered on the strings by a felt drum-

Example 6   'Arrival Platform Humlet' from *In a Nutshell*, selection of tunes.

stick (see Example 7). If we find the piece more effective and affecting than the *Hill Songs* the reason may be in part technical—the fluid rhythms and sonorities are more negotiable on Grainger's idiomatic piano that on collocations of wind instruments; and in part 'philosophical'—in that there is no pretence that man and nature may be identified. In this case the convoluted lines and harmonies may justly be called 'inspired', though not to the point of challenging Delius's sublime *Song of the High Hills*.

As a baring of the soul this uneasy 'Pastoral' is another Percy-paradox in the context of the suite, the last movement of which yanks us back from Grainger's most introverted piece to the lowest common denominator of common folk in Australia, with whom Percy is happy to identify. 'Gumsuckers' March' is so called because the inhabitants of Melbourne, where Percy was born, were known as gumsuckers—the gum being natural eucalyptus leaves, not the American commercial brands. There is no trace of condescension in the cocky tune, brash sonorities, and insouciant harmonies, which, in the piano versions, must be tackled con brio, and not too accurately. A second theme quotes the *Colonial Song* which Grainger intended as a national anthem for his native land, and it may not be an accident that the key of the march is traditionally heavenly E major, which is wishful-thinking, but touching. The Australianism of the march is affiliated by way of its ragtime flavour both to the Old World in the shape of Edwardian music-hall and to the New World in its incipient jazziness. A flutter of vulnerability is imparted to Grainger's self-vaunting democracy in that the final version of the march is dated 1914, on the eve of the Great War that was to destroy Australian innocence, as well as ours.

The war, we have noted, precipitated the Graingers' migration to America, where Percy landed up in, or at least on the periphery of, the armed forces. His job as an American military bandsman bore compositional fruit, for several of his later 'originals' were written for the band he directed. One of them, *Children's March: Over the Hills and Far Away*, was sketched in 1916 and fully worked out in 1918, scored for the normal wind-band plus piano. This suggests compromise between the military and the theatrical, and makes for a delectable, remarkably original piece. Having little to do with folk music, it is 'popular' both because of its military connotations and because of latent associations with American show-business music, retrospectively mated with English

Example 7 'Pastoral' from *In a Nutshell*, ending, piano version.

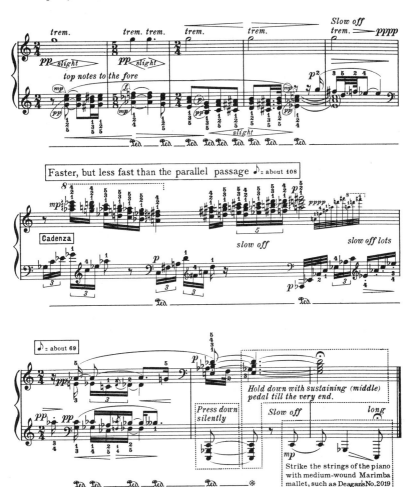

music-hall. More profoundly, it is popular in being genuinely childlike in spirit, as was its composer: as is immediately evident in the work's opening in a 'fairly fast', lolloping 6/8 march-rhythm, the key being pastoral F major, with a tune that is often 'childishly' pentatonic. Despite the regularity of the beat, the tune is often marked 'feelingly', for these kiddies have the heart of the matter in them. Little chromatic counter-themes dovetail into the main tune, in which the pentatonic thirds grow clownish, the

41

knockabout farce of their di-DA di-DA rhythm being more redolent of music-hall than of folksong (see Example 8). Although the chromatic counter-motives get stronger, the bumpkin simplicity of the main tune persists as, growing incrementally louder, the music modulates in a cycle of descending fifths from F to B flat, to E flat, to A flat. By this time the jollity is uproarious, with hints of Sousa march and American collegiate rag, refashioned in Grainger's rippingly boyish effervescence. At the apex of A flat merriment the music blows up in whirling scales in contrary motion, recalling the piccolo skirls in military music, and perhaps the baton-twirling marching maestro. From this point the procession recedes, declining in dynamics and retracing the steps of tonality back up the cycle of fifths, but stopping at B flat. Failure to return to the original F leaves the march in suspension; perhaps it even becomes an anti-military march in that these guileless children, following Pied Piper Percy, tramp over the hills and *far away*—from the nasty industrial world to Grainger's antipodal utopia. It is a joy to march with them; and one may have a comparable elevating experience in playing the (much-shortened) piano version to oneself, if one can momentarily feel as Puckish as Percy. Most liberating of all, perhaps, is the two-piano version, which is obstreperously physical—the cross-glissando explosion at the apex of the procession delivers a punch to the solar plexus—while being glintingly clear in its multiple polyphonies.

A smaller but related piece from Grainger's army years is *The*

Example 8 *Children's March: Over the Hills and Far Away*, two piano version, p.5, bass line.

*Immovable Do*, so called because it was originally improvised on a harmonium with a ciphering high C. Perhaps taking a cue from Purcell's *Fantasia on one note*, of which he'd recently made an arrangement, Grainger built this piece around a high C as inverted pedal, working it out between 1933 and 1940, in elastic scoring for military band or mixed wordless chorus, or for solo piano. It is most effective in the wind-band version, wherein shifting concords in moderate march-time produce an effect of open-eared wonderment similar to that of the *Children's March*. A third work, begun in 1918 but not finished until 1943, comes into this post-military category, but is more problematical. Its odd title, *The Power of Rome and the Christian Heart*, refers to the two European traditions—the classical State and the Christian Church—which Grainger so mistrusted, but also expresses a conflict between his basic pacifism and the patriotism that, he believed, also animated him. In particular it concerns the individual (himself) trying to survive in an alien world, preserving his native sensibility against the oppression of Rome or Christ or what- or whom-ever. The twelve-minute piece proves oddly disturbing, and demandingly difficult in its polyphonic and polychromatic scoring for large forces—choirs of flutes, oboes, bassoons, clarinets, saxophones, horns, and brass; batteries of orthodox and unorthodox percussion; a 'gamelan' of 'tuneful percussion'; pianos and harps at will, the more the merrier; and an important part for pipe or electric organ, unafraid of maximum vibrato. The textures alternate between stark diatonic severity and oleaginous chromaticism, in rhythms that are now powerfully monumental, now querulously pathetic. One feels that the piece might be impressive, without being sure whether its technical dubieties convince as evidence of a divided state of mind (which is what the work is about), or whether their divisiveness amounts to an evasion of artistic responsibility. It seems that Grainger himself wasn't sure, for although he worked on the piece for nearly thirty years (it was his last published work), he none the less said of it, after a performance by the prestigious Goldman Band at the Carnegie Hall in 1948: 'I loathed every note. I hated its commonplace chords, its oily wellsoundingness, its meaningless tonelines. My tonery has been growing more and more commonplace ever since I was about 20 or 22.' Although Grainger was right in associating inspiration with his youth, he was too rash in thus dismissing the 'wellsoundingness' of his mature years which, after all, embrace some of his finest music, including the magnificent *Lincolnshire Posy*. Perhaps, in *The Power of Rome*, he was defeated by the contrariety of his feelings. The work is seldom if ever heard, but deserves revival since its problematical nature is fundamental to the Grainger experience.

Whatever problems Grainger had with original composition vanished when he had already-existent music—folk, or traditional, or even another composer's—to trigger him off. It is therefore appropriate to end this chapter on his original music with a piece that is in fact original, while pretending to be a folk, or at least a 'traditional', song. *Colonial Song* was first sketched out in 1905—again that critical year—but wasn't seriously worked on until 1912–13, when it was dished up for two (optional) wordless voices, three strings, harp, and piano. Versions for piano trio with or without the voices, for piano solo with or without the voices, for military band, and for theatre orchestra followed between 1913 and 1928. The manifold versions hint at the significance the work had for Grainger as a deliberate attempt to create a quasi-folksong for his native land: white settlers' music having nothing to do, of course, with Aborigine music and democratically unabashed by the white settlers' rawness and sentimentality. As we have noted in commenting on 'Gumsuckers' March', Grainger shared in these qualities—and in the course of the march pointedly quotes a phrase from *Colonial Song*, his National Anthem for his antipodal home. It was therefore the more shattering when Sir Thomas Beecham, who had encouraged Percy to write *The Warriors*, notoriously dismissed *Colonial Song* as 'the worst orchestral piece of modern times'. Percy not only abandoned his idea of making *Colonial Song* the first of a series of 'Sentimentals'; he also decided that its tune was 'poor and clumsy', though he regretted that the great maestro hadn't entertained the possibility that it might be appropriate to the people and land it had been designed to celebrate.

To us at this date it seems a marvellous tune, in hopefully heavenly E major treated, as in Grainger's wont in longer pieces, in incremental variation. Each variation is more sumptuously harmonized until, after a no-holds-barred climax, the process is reversed, the dynamics being gradually subdued. The re-entry of the wordless voices for the coda is pure magic, and the chromatic harmony induces awe (see Example 9). We have to accept this music on Grainger's own, which are the Common Man's, terms, playing it in a style 'rich, broad and vibrating, with ample swells'. Its poignancy springs from the contrast between the quasi-pentatonic simplicity of its melody and its reverberant chromatic harmony, with clinging suspended seconds and gut-wrenching shifts to mediants. Communal hymn-singing and bleating suburban cornet solos create a scene in memory and love, while the 'national' aspects are manifest in the music's amplitude. As Grainger put it:

Perhaps it is not unnatural that people living more or less lonelily in vast virgin countries and struggling against natural and climatic hardships (rather than against the more actively and dramatically exciting counter wills of their fellow men, as in most thickly populated lands), should run largely to that persistently yearning, inactive sentimental wistfulness that we find so touchingly expressed in much American art: for instance in Mark Twain's *Huckleberry Finn* and in Stephen C. Foster's adorable songs, *My Old Kentucky Home*, *The Old Folks at Home* etc. I have also noticed curious, almost Italian-like tendencies in brass-band performances and ways of singing in Australia (such as a preference for richness and intensity of tone and soulful breadth of phrasing over more subtly and sensitively handled delicacies of expression) which are also reflected here.

Grainger is telling us that, if *Colonial Song* is sublimated kitsch, that is a commodity essential to our spiritual survival in a

Example 9   *Colonial Song*, piano version, pp. 10–11.

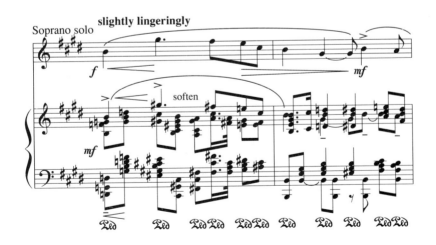

45

Example 9  *cont.*

46

commodity-dealing community. That the sophisticatedly mercurial Sir Thomas Beecham Bt. should find it 'vulgar' is not surprising, but to dismiss it on those grounds was unworthy of his rapier-edged intelligence, for what else but vulgar, in both the strict and the colloquial sense, could or should it have been? In this instance the musical Grand Seigneur was less wise than the Boy from the Bush.

# 3
# DANCING WITH THE HAPPY TRIBES
## *Grainger and the Human Body*

That *Colonial Song* was an original that pretended to be folk, trad, or pop music takes us to the core of Grainger's work which, despite his egocentricity and his identification with Nordic outsiders like Delius, was centred on communal rather than personal consciousness. Ultimate among his paradoxes is the fact that he had to lose the self in order to find it: as was already implicit in his aborted search for Nature not anthropomorphically, but 'in herself'. In the light of this we may understand why his ultimate favourite composer was not after all, Delius but Bach, who might almost be considered Delius's polar opposite.

This Percy-paradox has, however, its topsy-turvey logic. Grainger was enraptured by Delius because, an heir to Wagner, he had been *through* 'Europe'. The essence of Delius's music is the flux of sensation—the sighing of Wagnerian appoggiaturas within the chromatic woof of the mammoth nineteenth-century symphony orchestra, itself a paradoxical product of industrial technology. Even so, all the component strands of Delius's music *sing* and are, individually considered, vocal and often modal in contour. In the orchestral and choral *Song of the High Hills* the rhapsodic melodies incline to pentatonicism, like so much folk-song, as though they were seeking a oneness beyond the flux. The celebration of the sensual life in and for itself leads to a desire to lose the self in the supposedly simpler satisfactions of a lost youth, and above all in the contemplation of Nature's impersonal hills and sea; for the passion is too strong to be borne. The theme of Delius's finest opera—again written at the turn of the century—is that while passion is the only reality, the sham that passes for reality renders passion untenable. The ideal love of the adolescent Village Romeo and Juliet, like that of grown-up Tristan and Isolde, can find consummation only in Lethean oblivion, beneath the waters of those significantly titled Paradise Gardens.

The relation between this Delian experience and the adolescent Grainger at the time of his exactly contemporary *Hill Songs* is

48

patent. Grainger, however, was too young and too buoyant for Delian nostalgia; and could complementarily relish in Bach a composer who had never needed to lose the self because, as a man of faith, he had never been under its thrall. Percy said that he fell in love with Bach's music at the same time (aged 10) as he discovered Anglo-Saxon and Old Norse sagas; having grown up, he could see the connection between these two creative acts. It was Bach's (sagalike?) 'long flow form that I fell in love with, whereas folksong did not reach me for more than ten years after discovering Bach. Of all the music that I heard in Germany, the first chorus of Bach's *Matthew Passion* was the most satisfying, and even today it is still my favourite piece of music—such glorious lengths, all that lovely muddle'. Basically, Grainger found in Bach the 'going-onness' and 'long flow form' that he so relished in the dance-songs of Faroe Islanders and in the improvised choral polyphony of the Polynesian ritual singers he heard in 1912. The latter he compared to Bach: who significantly has proved congenial to and exploitable by black jazz musicians, and, to a lesser degree, by white urban rock bands. Grainger revelled in some tribal musics, in much jazz (especially Duke Ellington's) and in most Nordic folk-song and dance precisely because they were bigger than the self, if not as big as Bach. In this sense Bach, for all his technical sophistication, fostered Grainger's love of the common touch, and even chimed with his ventures into sea-music, bush-music, and train-music, all of which were dedicated to things 'beyond' the self. Grainger's musical geography is here again pertinent

I realize that the small fields, or broken-up geography of such countries as Italy, Austria, Germany and England make for small conceptions of form and the wish for constant contrast. It is only natural that English and German composers should have what I consider a 'bijou' conception of musical form, while an Australian should have a continental conception (and *such* a continent, so grandly monotonous, uneventful, and unbroken-up).

Of course Percy excepted Bach from these strictures on German music—and might have excepted Bruckner, had he been familiar with his symphonies. The gospel he is preaching is minimalist before its time. Musical content is not dependent on, and may be in inverse proportion to, mere size, though one can understand why, at the time, Grainger felt it necessary to play down

49

'consciousness'. We may be grateful that—unlike some of today's minimalists and many of yesterday's punk musicians—he did not make a deliberate cult of vacuity.

But of course Bach himself was hardly a minimalist; there is a 'European' angle to his work that more deeply if less overtly appealed to Grainger who, after all, worked within European traditions. Although Percy detected analogies between Bach and his improvising Polynesians, he was more accurate when he related their heterophonic choralism to the twelfth-century Perotin. Despite Percy's charming phrase, the first chorus of the *Matthew Passion* is not in fact a 'lovely muddle', though that might be acceptable as a description of Perotin's and the Polynesians' polyphony. Bach stands central in European history because he simultaneously embraces the post-Renaissance, European sense of temporal progression and a non-Western, or at least pre-Renaissance, timelessness. Technically, this is manifest in his music's equilibrium between the horizontal (linear-polyphonic) and the vertical (harmonic-homophonic) dimensions. For Grainger, Bach was a 'total man' in the faithful certitudes of his continuous lines, consistent figurations, and incremental rhythms, combined with a harmonic progression that, through the *as-though* preordained order of counterpoint, could still be an antidote to the wilful egoism he mistrusted in the Viennese classics. We may find his attitude to Beethoven infantile, but his appreciation of Bach showed the highest intuitive intelligence.

This intelligence extends to Grainger's Bach being his own Bach, not the one traditionally accepted. For Percy, who as a child played Bach with unflagging zest, the German was not the supreme composer of the Christian Cross, which the adult Grainger, along with Delius, abominated. Such human fallibilities as compassion, conscience, and guilt were also tossed out when Grainger, confessing to truly global pluralism, wrote to Rose in 1911:

I have no feeling for purity, honesty and holiness, but I admire INTENSITY & WILL NOT be left behind by the Christians and Puritans. We must try to combine all, the body of the English, the self-discipline of the Jews, the sexual wealth of niggers, the broad good heart of the Germans, the spiritual sympatheticness of the Scandinavians, the thoroughness of the French, the humanity of the old Greeks, the brutality of the Romans, the Passionateness of the Christians and the pluckiness of these American mind-cults.

He might even have made out a case that Bach's 'universal' art embraced many if not all of these elements; certainly he enshrined Bach as the nonpareil among composers because, without bypassing the 'European' awareness of passion, pain, and death, he affirmed life so abundantly. Bach's all-inclusiveness must have been the reason why in the long run Percy got more from Bach than he did from his Polynesian 'savages' though he might have been reluctant to admit this, as a matter of principle.

In respect to Bach, one might even say that Grainger's inconsistencies and illogicalities were evidence of his intuitive intelligence; he knew, as most people wouldn't have known, that his devotion to Bach had a crucial relation to his fervour over folk music. As so often, he was cavalier about dates when he stated that he had no interest in folk-song until ten years after he had been bowled over by Bach. He produced a sheaf of folk-song settings as early as 1898–9, and in the following year made fourteen brief arrangements of 'Songs of the North'. Folk-like qualities were to a degree manifest in the boyishness of his juvenile music, and in its corporeality. When, early in his career, Percy discovered his composing identity, it was by way of his Bachian body-rhythms, for the tie-up between Bach and the Folk is most patent and potent in Grainger's settings of dance tunes. These owe their durability, and perhaps their popularity, to their Bach-like continuity of beat, consistency of figuration, and interdependence between 'horizontal' line and 'vertical' harmony. They start from the physical rather than the metaphysical aspects of Bach's art and, in their relatively simple way, are proudly affirmatory. While no-one would claim that Grainger's dances have the musical substance of Bach's English and French Suites or his Partitas, let alone the polyphonic-homophonic density of the Brandenburg Concertos, there are valid parallels between Grainger's instrumental—especially keyboard—techniques and those of Bach. This is why even Grainger's 'light' dances, which became commercial assets in later life, have preserved their liveliness through so many, sometimes indifferent, performances. This applies whether the pieces are dishings up of traditional tunes, as are *Shepherd's Hey, Country Gardens,* and *Molly on the Shore,* or whether, like *Mock Morris* and *Handel in the Strand,* they are originals cast in traditional style.

*Shepherd's Hey* is a real folk-dance tune that Grainger took down from the playing of three fiddlers of the Bidford Morris dance-team in 1906. He dished it up for piano in 1908, and later made versions for military band and for 'room-music 12-some', consisting of flute, clarinet, horn, concertina, and eight strings. In its original form on Bidford village green *Shepherd's Hey* was, of course, functional music for dancing to, consisting of an 8 + 8 bar tune in straight G major, repeated as many times as were necessary to complete the formal pattern, or simply until the dancers were tired. Grainger makes a piano piece to play in the home or even at a concert, but doesn't change the music's functional nature, since he merely repeats the tune five times, differently scored but with only slight harmonic variation. The first half of the first statement could be played by two folk fiddlers, and is perhaps transcribed from the original performance; their dancing interplay, intermittently crossing one another, transfers effectively to keyboard (see Example 10). The answering 'eight' accompanies the tune in treble register with clearly spaced homophony such as could be played by other strings and/or concertina; extra parts insert an occasional frisk above the tune, for this music is of its essence corporeal. Next time round the tune is in alto register, but there is always at least one other part with melodic identity, thereby reminding us that a community is an aggregate of individual human creatures.

In the next statement the tune is pawkily in the bass, and

Example 10   *Shepherd's Hey*, opening, piano solo version.

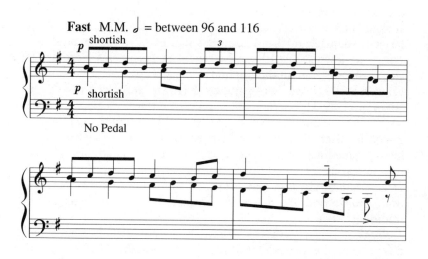

acquires energy from modulations (to the dominant and to A minor) that don't disturb the cheery diatonicism. Suddenly soft, the next variation gives greater prominence to a cantabile counter-melody in an inner part than to the tune itself, textures now being 'smooth and clinging'. The remaining statements are all exuberant, with the tune bouncing between treble and bass, while the tempo gets faster and faster. This is a traditional way whereby dancers may bring momentum to an end; here the final glissando is an 'all fall down'. So this piece functions more on the habits of communal activity than on accredited artistic principles, though there is excellent art in the Bachian way in which theme and its counter-themes dance over the keyboard, in the Bach-like clarity of line and consistency of figuration, and in the life-affirming pulse. Small wonder that this simple dance does not tarnish, either in the piano version or in the small-orchestra version in which the instruments preserve, or re-create, vernal folk sonorities.

*Shepherd's Hey* is a transcription of a genuine folk fiddle tune that, turned into 'art', preserves something of the orgiastic effect of folk performance; it is not, or at least it is more than, a concert piece. That such was Grainger's normal approach to composition is indicated if we compare the piano version of *Shepherd's Hey* with that of the *Walking Tune* 'worked out and scored in 1905'. This piece too was functional music in that Grainger had 'made it up on a three-days' walk in the Scottish Highlands in 1900, as a hummed accompaniment to my tramping feet'. This was the famous Highland jaunt that had inspired the *Hill Songs*, and the original scoring of the *Walking Tune* for 'wind five-some' (flute, oboe, clarinet, horn, and bassoon) may have been intended to emulate the 'wild' noises he'd heard from those rustic pipers. In association with a simple, symmetrical, folk-like tune, however, the piece has little in common with the rhapsodic *Hill Songs*, sounding sprightly, but pastorally benign. In the piano version we discover that although *Walking Tune* is an original whereas *Shepherd's Hey* is a transcription, each works in the same way. At first the tune for walking to carols blithely in the top line, accompanied by four other real parts derived from the original wind quintet, though parts may occasionally drop out, or may be added in cadences. The structure is again 8 + 8, the first strain sometimes being stretched to ten bars, with an extended cadence. The tune is in straight G major, but one may be tempted to call it the

Ionian mode on G, for the prevalent fourths and fifths in the contours of the melody give it a folkily pentatonic flavour. The second clause is less openly expansive, hemmed in by repeated notes and sequences, though the hummed tune stays content. There is no real modulation, only a couple of chromatic passing notes.

As in *Shepherd's Hey*, the first statement of the tune is followed by a varied repeat merrily in the higher octave, with wider spacing between the parts and therefore with more polyphonic independence. The chromatic F natural this time produces a modulation to the subdominant, but the effect is fleeting. The second clause, with its repeated notes, is not however treated strictly, for both inner and under parts are chromaticized, and fragments of tune tend to get bogged in their repetitiveness. Inability to break away perhaps encourages enhanced chromaticism when the tune lifts up an octave, and there is a real modulation to the relative, E minor. Through two-bar chromatic sequences the tune undulates 'lingeringly', and the lingering may have a functional relationship to the tramper's flagging footsteps. Atypically of Grainger, this meandering middle section has remote affinities with the development section of a sonata movement—except that its effect is anti-developmental! Even so, there is a recapitulation after the music has wound its way back—by way of a 'slacken lots' (Grainger's blue-eyed English for molto ritenuto)—to G major. The two clauses of the original tune are repeated in the original scoring and in the first 'gently flowing' tempo. The repeat in the high octave is extended and enriched, with the tune in canon between treble and tenor. This flows into a coda 'very very slightly slower', in exquisitely dovetailed polyphony that looks, and even sounds, like a tranquil Bach chorale prelude (see Example 11). Once more, quite high art has been distilled from primitive functionalism; even the fairly sophisticated structure, with its hint of sonata form, has functional implications in relation to the weary walker. The jazzy added sixth in the G major chord distances the walker from Time's pendulum; maybe he naps while trudging along. Nothing could be further from Grainger's musical philosophy than the doctrine of Art for Art's sake. Everything he wrote was for people's sake—other people's, even more than his own.

Grainger's other well-known dances all come into a category defined either by *Shepherd's Hey* or by *Walking Tune*, or by some compromise between them. The most famous of them, *Country*

Example 11　*Walking Tune*, piano version, p.10.

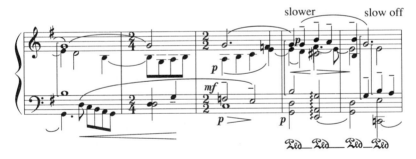

*Gardens*, is a genuine morris dance which Percy lighted on in a published collection and rough-sketched in straight diatonic E flat major 'for whistlers and a few instruments' in 1908. He didn't work it out as a piano piece until 1918, during his army years, when he was delighted that the lads in the band so relished it, though he later deplored its ubiquity. What carried *Country Gardens* so effortlessly to the Top of the Grainger Pops is a shade mysterious. Basically, credit must go to the Folk for a tune so irresistibly catchy in line and bouncy in rhythm; yet it was none the less Grainger who made the tune—which after all had been around a long time—a 'household word' in an environment very different from that which had made it. His modern–urban–democratic approach makes for a new kind of People's Music in which communal and personal identity merge. His wide-open keyboard spacing, the swing he imparts to both the bounding pulse and the bucolic boogie of the dotted rhythm, the artful inner chromatics and the increasingly cheeky harmonization of the repeats communicate so physical a glee that our smiles of pleasure may break into overt giggles or guffaws. We personally relish Percy's personal contribution; such is his generosity of spirit that we may even kid ourselves into thinking that we've made it ourselves. That may be one definition of 'folk' music and is certainly a by-no-means trivial aspect of Grainger's genius—more important than the aboriginality of the *Hill Songs*, if less significant than the re-creation of folk-songs (rather than dances) that we'll be considering in the next two chapters.

Grainger's rustic peasants, in their 'days of yore', must have displayed comparably physical reactions to the dancing moment. No doubt they introduced personal quirks into communal gallivanting, or broke into spontaneous whistles as they capered; Grainger's partiality for whistlers probably springs from the fact that their exuberance releases the breath of life totally without self-consciousness. *Molly on the Shore* is more sophisticated than *Country Gardens*, showing considerable technical ingenuity in combining two traditional reels again extracted from a printed source and set in many forms, beginning with strings in 1907, and proceeding through piano, two pianos, wind-band, theatre orchestra, and finally, in 1949, full orchestra for a Stokowski recording. With *Molly* we marvel not so much at the comicality of Grainger's invention as at the artfulness with which the diatonic major tunes are interlaced, and the fleet-footed canter of the metre(s). This is another meeting between spontaneous physical zest and an artifice that is itself a release from selfhood—which may have been why Percy made a version of the piece for a mechanical but blithely babbling pianola.

Just as the real folk dance *Shepherd's Hey* is complemented by the pretend folk dance Percy called *Walking Tune*, so the real reels of *Molly on the Shore* are balanced by the *Mock Morris*, begun in 1910 and passing through as many versions as *Molly* between that date and 1952. This is precisely what its title suggests: a *mock* morris dance in which 'no folk-music tune-stuffs at all are used'. Although the rhythmic cast of the piece is morris-like, 'neither the build of the tune nor the general layout of the form keeps to the Morris dance shape'. Indeed, the origins of the piece are urban, for 'the tune came to me in bed, the morning after seeing *The Arcadians*', and may be construed as homage to George Grossmith and his famous ditty, 'I've got a motter, Always merry and bright'. The collusion of 'motter' (motto) with 'Mother' and with music-hall was naturally irresistible to Percy, though he doesn't quote the *tune* of Grossmith's number. What's remarkable about the piece is that it simultaneously functions as urban entertainment and as 'mock' bucolic revelry, and convinces on both counts.

Edwardian music-hall is behind *Handel in the Strand* too, though it is also described as a clog dance. The original version of 1911–12 was for piano, violin, optional viola, cello, or 'massed pianos and strings'. Later, in 1930, and then in 1952 for the Stokowski recording, Grainger dished it up again for piano solo and larger orchestras. The Strand in the title explicitly points to the music-hall, while the reference to Handel indicates that early sketches incorporated bits of Handel's well-known *Harmonious Blacksmith* variations. There is a bridge between Handel's Vauxhall Gardens and Edwardian London: which again suggests compromise between once-aristocratic art and proletarian entertainment. The agility of the rhythms and the polyphonic-harmonic lucidity of the textures continue to lift hearts as well as to set feet tapping. This is why this 'light' music has outlived so much of the heavier variety.

In their theatre-orchestra versions Grainger's dances invite active participation; he preferred *Handel in the Strand* to be danced to, clogs and all. In their piano versions, which not-so-many years ago were widely current in domestic parlours, they afford even more pleasure when played to oneself than when passively listened to—though passivity is hard to come by when arms and legs are set instinctively twitching. A few of Grainger's dance pieces, more ambitious than the famous numbers discussed above, amount to 'performance music' in a different and more complex sense. Especially remarkable is the *Scotch Strathspey and Reel* which, 'inlaid with several Scots and Irish tunes and a Sea-shanty', was first sketched out for 'band with strings' in 1901; was scored for '4-part men and room-music 20-some (21 or 22 at will)' in 1911; and was rehashed as a virtuoso piano piece in

1927–8. In one passage of the orchestral version '6 Scotch and Irish tunes are heard together, along with "What shall we do with a drunken sailor?"' The first strathspey tune introduced is the 'Marquis of Huntley', in the Dorian mode on G, with vivaciously fiddling syncopations and a quasi-plucked-string accompaniment with Lydian sharp fourths. Cantabile inner themes creep in through the pervasively pentatonic formulations, and the accompaniment subsides in sequential sevenths to approach the cadences. This tune merges into an 'ancient Irish clan-march' in Mixolydian, or perhaps Lydian, G: and that in turn proves to be an embryonic form of the Drunken Sailor's shanty, at first bellowed robustly, but with a somewhat sinister, growling coda in sequential sevenths. All these tunes intertwine, and garner others, moving to a climax by way of 'skirling' bagpipes in top register (see Example 12). The 'Reel of Tulloch' becomes itself a climax by being in Mixolydian G over a bagpipe drone. The majorish feeling impels the music irresistibly forward to a babel of screeching piccolos: which are not merely to be listened to, but to be acted out audibly, and perhaps terpsichoreanly! For these interlac-

Example 12  *Scotch Strathspey and Reel*, piano version, p.9.

58

ing textures are not merely musical, though they are that; they also create the social context—the rowdy pub or obstreperous dance-hall—wherein these events occur.

Grainger was aware of what he was doing, for he writes:

If a roomfull of Scottish and Irish fiddlers and pipers and any nationality of English-speaking, shanty-singing, deep-sea sailors could be miraculously spirited together and suddenly endowed with the gift of polyphonic improvisation . . . what a strange, merry, friendly babel of tune, harmony and rhythm might result! My setting of *Strathspey and Reel* mirrors the imagination of such a contingency.

We may hear this on Benjamin Britten's celebrated disc, *Salute to Percy Grainger*, which includes a performance of *Strathspey and Reel* presumably based on Grainger's room-music set-up, but with the shanty yelled by raucous male voices. Grainger would have been delighted by a performance that is a miniature tone-poem, deeply moving as well as sensually and alcoholically inspiriting. As the tipsy voices swell and fade through the smoke-laden haze, the effect of the sequential seventh passage becomes distinctly minatory.

This is more 'poetic' than Martin Jones's dazzling caper through the virtuoso piano version. Although Grainger said that the 'polyphonic conglomeration' of the room-music version couldn't be accommodated on a single piano, his keyboard version makes a bold shot at it. The sheer legerdemain increases the sense of danger; we embark on a riotous binge that is pianistically far removed from Liszt. Grainger's keyboard acrobatics carry us with him into the thick of the mêlée. The difficulty is not, like Liszt's, exhibitionistic, for it precipitates action rather than calling attention to itself. The pentatonic tune, at first luminously laid out on the keyboard, doesn't prepare us for the riot to come as other tunes, including the roistering sea-shanty, incrementally intrude. The orchestral version (as presented by Britten) and the piano solo version (as played by Martin Jones) are very different, yet each is magnificent and has its own authenticity.

A similarly communal dance piece, *Spoon River*, is based on American, not British, material. Originally set as a piano piece in 1919, shortly after Grainger had become an American citizen, it was dished up for two pianos in 1922, and in 1929 was re-presented in elastic scoring ranging from three instruments to full orchestra. The elasticity hints that Grainger hoped the piece might be social music wherever two or three or a hundred were gathered together: as was the case with the American country fiddlers who originally played the tunes. The work wasn't, however, inspired by Grainger's attendance at a folk-fiddle session but by a tune noted down in 1857 by a Captain Charles H. Robinson. Many years later it came into the hands of Edgar Lee Masters, poet of the *Spoon River Anthology*, the verses of which deal with the lives of Poor Whites in the South. Masters knew Grainger because the latter admired his verses. He passed on Capt. Robinson's tune to Percy, who added a few other country fiddle tunes and made up a few of his own, producing a work that distilled the 'lonesome wistfulness and sturdy persistence' of a nearly vanished world. Grainger's (longer) version for two pianos is especially beautiful, for the medium allows scope for his clean-spaced harmonic polyphony, with spellbinding effect. This would seem to imply that although the music is presently active in dancing bodies and fiddling arms, it is also retrospective, and to that degree consciously artistic. The two-piano version is comparatively late in date, published in the United States in 1932.

Another American dance piece, *In Dahomey*, dating from Grainger's most creative years 1903–9, unusually exists in only one version, for piano solo. This is not surprising since it is Grainger's quintessential piece of piano virtuosity, 'a wonderfully jazzy romp' (as John Pickard puts it in his liner notes to Jones's CD performance), 'which would surely have established instant popularity were it not so horrendously difficult to play'. The title refers to a 'Darkie Comic Opera' by Will Marion Cook, and embraces other material from minstrel shows and 'Coon Band Contests'. Grainger subtitled it 'Cakewalk Smasher', and smash it does, in the style of the dance fantasias of the early nineteenth-century New Orleans piano virtuoso Louis-Moreau Gottschalk, who was an even more outrageous showman than Grainger. (Not even Percy lived for some months in the Andes, on a rock projecting over an extinct volcano, trundling out his grand piano every evening to give a recital to the immense forests, waving savannahs, gibbering monkeys, and howling jaguars.) Musically, Gottschalk was elegant in his Creole-Franco-German-Jewish romanticism; comparatively, Grainger's piece swashbuckles in rip-roaring fiesta, adrift in what eighteenth-century Dr Burney called 'extravagant and licentious modulations', and as riotously abandoned as a New Orleans honky-tonk pianist, note-clusters, double glissandos, warts and all. A performer today—even a Martin Jones—can hardly avoid a generous sprinkle of wrong notes, and these wrong notes are right. In many ways Grainger's Cakewalk is 'later' than Gottschalk's; no trace of European glamour survives here, any more than it does in the ragtime movements in Ives's piano sonatas. A New World, more barbarous than the old, brings the house down, and we're thrilled to collapse with it.

*In Dahomey* is a somewhat rare phenomenon, an unambiguously *pagan* fiesta created by a man reared, on the whole, within 'Western' traditions. It has nothing to do with Bach's 'long flow form' but, in its rumbustious immediacy, attests to Percy's conviction that 'all our dark and needless belief in sin stems from religion, while our disastrous ambitions stem from the fighting spirit of the Old Testament. The world of modern doctoring, modern machines, modern art, modern amorality would be just paradise if we could only shed the blight of religion.' What a strange statement from a man who revered Bach above all composers; yet how consistent it is with a man who professed to live in thrall to the body. But we've already noted evidence enough of Percy's paradoxical inconsistencies. If much of his music celebrated the human body, as much or more celebrated the human voice, in-spired with the breath of life. This music is the subject of our next chapter.

# 4

# SINGING WITH THE HAPPY TRIBES

## Grainger and the Human Voice

During the year 1932–3, when he was devising his course at the New York College of Arts, Grainger was even more than usually fertile in ideas about music's nature and purpose. Many of them were brilliant, some were near-lunatic, and few were carried through to a coherent end, being vitiated by his lack of formal education and perhaps by a basic incapacity for consecutive thought. One of his madder notions was published as an article in an American periodical called *Music News*, in September 1933. Under the title of 'Melody versus Rhythm' the article tries to establish a dichotomy between melody (free, unfettered, overriding time) as a manifestation of 'positive' emotions like love, compassion, and tenderness; and rhythm (time-dominated, bar-measured) as a manifestation of the will, conducive to inhumane, if not inhuman, 'negative' emotions like competitiveness and domination. This dichotomy is not entirely meaningless. Looking back on the history of European music one can observe that 'horizontal' music, whether in terms of unaccompanied melody as in plainsong, or in terms of medieval organum and heterophony, or of Renaissance polyphony, has tended to encourage 'spiritual' values: whereas 'vertical' music, whether in the dance-dominated homophony of the Baroque eras or in the Classical sonata-music of the eighteenth and nineteenth centuries, has been associated with the imposition of the will, often in autocratic forms. Where Grainger went wrong, rendering his case absurd, was in adopting an either–or attitude: as no less a musician than Bartók pointed out in penning a riposte to Percy's article. It may be true, Bartók explained, that to a degree melody 'represents' the human spirit, while rhythm represents the body. None the less the two, being interdependent, cannot exist without one another; and this applies alike to musical techniques and to human life in the process of living it. What makes Grainger's case the more untenable is that his theory is contradicted by his own practice. As we have seen in the last chapter, a substantial core of his work can be described as 'body-music'; and as we will see in this chapter, one can draw no clearly defined line between this body-music, founded on the dance, and the no-less substantial part of Grainger's music which is 'spiritually' rooted in (vocally derived) singing line. What Grainger called 'beatless music' was not really without beat, though it was subtle, even complex, in rhythmic organization. He found prototypes for this 'spiritual' melody in the singing of the agrarian folk whose tunes he collected; and he was justified in believing that their songs served as ballast not only against what Yeats called 'the fury and the mire of human veins', but specifically against the oppressive materialism of the modern world—against Matthew Arnold's 'darkling plain | Swept with confused alarms of struggle and flight | Where ignorant armies clash by night'.

In adopting this social, latently moralistic, approach to folk-song Grainger was in tune with British revivalists such as Vaughan Williams and Cecil Sharp, though he did not know them intimately. He met Vaughan Williams occasionally to take photographs of his beautiful blue eyes to add to his collection of blue-eyed heroes. Sharp he regarded as a pedagogic archaeologist with little understanding of the spirit of folksong, though he must have admitted to some value in Sharp's researches since he offered to donate half his considerable earnings from *Country Gardens* to foster the work of Sharp's Folksong Society (Sharp died before this offer could be implemented). Far more significant, however, in Grainger's rediscovery of 'folk conscious-ness' was Edvard Grieg: partly because he came from a small Nordic country still relatively untouched by what Percy consid-ered the blight of industrialization, and partly because Grieg's childlike simplicity matched Percy's own, while being as gentle as his was fierce. In 1906, just after he'd embarked on his field-work in Lincolnshire, Grainger visited Norway from whence, having met Grieg, he wrote to tell his mother that, 'of all the composers who ever existed Grieg and Bach are the ones I love the most; and it was quite undescribable for me to see the tiny little bit of a person and to hear the music at the same time'. In the following year (1907) he wrote that 'the more I see of Norwegian art the more marvellous I think darling old Grieg. He has avoided all that social rising from the peasants upwards through the middle classes that is so tiresome. And his *volkskundlich* things are either genuinely folkish or *better in their own way.*' Grieg was no less appreciative of his young disciple, describing Percy as 'a young man of genius, possessing the real artist's soul. Although born in Melbourne, Australia, he talks Norwegian, and is full of enthusiasm for our land and art.' He was enraptured by Percy's performance of his piano concerto, played in so 'strikingly Norwegian a way, with all its wildness and delicate tenderness'.

As a musician, Grieg was pertinent to Grainger in both aspects of his (illusory) dichotomy between rhythm and melody, body and spirit. Grainger was especially partial to the piano arrangements of folk fiddle-dances collated in Grieg's opus 66 and opus 72, which he frequently included in his recitals. Grieg could barely credit that Grainger could play his *Slåtter* opus 72 as though he were momentarily metamorphosed into a Hardanger folk fiddler, scraping his instrument to produce sounds startlingly anticipatory of the folk-music arrangements of Bartók. These were to play a considerable part in Bartók's forging of an art-music appropriate to a Hungarian European of the twentieth century. Grieg's *Slåtter* are no less vividly 'environmental', and although smaller pieces than Grainger's *Strathspey and Reel*, are in the same sense 'performance music' that found its way into the drawing room. Grieg maintained that no Scandinavian pianist approached Grainger in presenting—making present—not merely the notes, but the sounds and ambiance, of the fiddle-dances he has pianistically reanimated in his opus 66 and opus 72.

But Grainger's debt to his beloved Grieg is evident in his treatment of songs as well as dances, and to this area the more intimate aspects of Grieg's piano music are relevant. His *Lyric Pieces*, published in ten volumes between 1867 and 1901, may be readily associated with the 'love, compassion and tenderness' which Percy associated with melody and spiritual values, for they are recollections of boyhood experience in his Nordic agrarian homeland, veering between nostalgic memories of folk life (and folk-songs) and the intimacies of the solitary heart. Often Grieg discovered the universal within the particular: with exquisite immediacy in pieces from the earlier volumes (the 'Arietta' from opus 12, the 'Berceuse' from opus 33, and the heart-breaking 'Melodie' from opus 47); and more profoundly in the later volumes ('Notturno' and 'Klokkeklang'—a bell piece—from opus 54, 'Secrecy' and 'Homesickness' from opus 57, 'Once upon a time', 'Gone', and

'Remembrance' from the last collection, opus 71). The titles themselves indicate the music's pervasive nostalgia, though it mattered to Grainger, as it matters to us, that the pieces look forward as well as back. When Emil Gilels somewhat surprisingly made a CD of Grieg's *Lyric Pieces* he paid tribute to the 'depths of tenderness and mystery' the unpretentious pieces contained, and pointed out how many of them anticipate Debussyan impressionism. Gilels' disc has become justly celebrated, demonstrating that 'little Grieg', as the pianist puts it, 'was part of a great tradition, formulating in musical terms the "truth" of the ever-seeking, solitary human being'. Listening to Gilels' performances one understands why Grainger, himself a 'lonely desert man', came to think of Grieg as a soul-mate. His smallness and truth were more within Percy's compass than the windswept grandeurs of his other Nordic hero, Delius. But Grainger's task was trickier than Grieg's in that he didn't belong to a self-enclosed agrarian society but was a homeless citizen of the wide world.

It may be this that gives his small folk-song settings their pathos; he loved folk-song *because* it sprang from regional roots and a stable home such as he, and modern industrial society, lacked. Percy's most frequently performed works may be the body-music dances, but the works closest to his heart are the folksong settings, for the basic reason that the song-tunes tend to plumb deeper than the dance-tunes. Especially Grieg-like are some of the brief folk-song arrangements for voice and piano or for piano solo, beginning with those collected on the famous Scottish trip with his mother in 1900. In 'Leezie Lindsay', 'Fair Young Mary', and 'Mo Nighean Dhu' he strikes just the right balance between the tune's simplicity and the emotiveness of his harmonic commentary. Many years later, in his introduction to a volume of 'easy pieces', he asked: 'Why should we harmonize folksongs at all?' since the folk never sing them with accompaniment and

most lovers of folksong will agree that a folksong never sounds so well as when it is sung wholly without harmony, by a genuine folksinger. In spite of all that, most of us composers feel an irresistible urge to harmonize (or polyphonize) folksongs—possibly because we like to wed our harmonies to REAL TUNES, real tunes being something that we modern composers seem unable to write ourselves.

Percy's reference to the poverty of modern melodic invention isn't a joke; it ties in with his association of melody with humanity and spirituality, and is implicit social criticism in that it supports his view that music in society won't flourish again until makers and doers once more join hands. This is also why Grainger adds that he tries to make his harmonies, however 'modern', accord with folk spirit in that his added 'tone-strands' are 'themselves somewhat folk-like, so that the total result may seem as if several folksongs were being played or sung together'. This 'musical democracy' inevitably introduces a new harmonic dimension: which makes sense since we aren't in fact agrarian folk. In his folk-song settings Grainger, like Grieg, looks back but also forward, in so far as his transcription is re-creation.

A lovely example is 'The Sussex Mummers' Christmas Carol', a tune taken down by Lucy Broadwood in 1880 and set for piano by Grainger in 1905, though it wasn't 'finished off' until 1911. The melody—it is more than a tune—begins with a noble rising fifth and, flowing in stepwise movement, generates an ineffable calm. The piece consists of two 'singings' of a ten-bar Ionian melody notated by Grainger as D flat major, moving in level crotchets. The tune, beginning in treble register, then wafting between alto and tenor, is harmonized homophonically, but with the independent 'tone-strands' twining in democratic togetherness. Approaching the cadence, Grainger flattens the seventh to effect a momentary but heart-easing modulation to the subdominant. Otherwise, he finds no need to introduce chromatics, the effect of warm security and serenity being produced by tender secundal suspensions and by the resonant spacing of the chords on the keyboard and beneath the hands (see Example 13). Frequently, the main melody is embedded in the middle of the texture, a technique which—as Ronald Stevenson has pointed out—is typical of improvised Negro choral singing. To this degree Grainger's harmonic thinking, as well as his polyphony, was rooted in folk practice: so that the ancient and modern aspects of his quasi-folk music need not be at odds. It's interesting, and superficially surprising, that Grainger himself did not make a version of this carol for unaccompanied voices, though he published versions wherein solo violin or cello pick out the main tune from the enveloping piano texture. At the end of his life he started a version for wind-band, which was finished by Richard Franko Goldman and published in 1965. The hymnic sonorities sound very fine on band, but are not real substitutes for the simultaneous intimacy and grandeur induced by the original solo

Example 13 'The Sussex Mummers' Christmas Carol', ending.

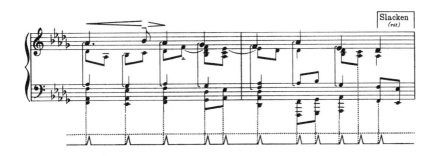

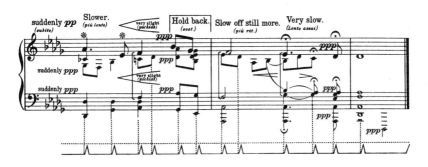

✳ The rhythm of these 2 notes is here altered by me. The original form is given in the first time through [(full) bar 9]. *P.A.G.*

piano. This piano score merits close attention; if one meticulously follows the composer's instructions as to voice-leading, dynamic range, and pedalling, one will learn much about the relationship between oral and literate traditions.

Grainger dedicated 'The Sussex Mummers' Christmas Carol',

along with the complete series of 'British Folk Music Settings', 'lovingly and reverently to the memory of Edvard Grieg', who died after the carol had been composed, but before it was published. The dedication was a general act of homage, not merely to Grieg as a composer of small piano pieces: for Grainger's vocal version of 'Brigg Fair'—possibly the most heart-rending setting of a folk-song ever made—is also an elegy for the Norwegian. Percy took the tune down in 1905, from his favourite Lincolnshire singer Joseph Taylor, arranging it in the following year for tenor solo and mixed chorus. The melody, in the Dorian mode on G, floats in gentle curves that promise love as the young man journeys, on a particularized 'fifth of August', to Brigg Fair, where he will meet his 'dear'. 'Up with the lark in the morning', his heart is happy yet vulnerable, as are life and love themselves. Grainger incorporates some of Taylor's melismatic ornamentation into the tune's undulating contours, giving it a touching immediacy related to the lover's hopeful-fearful state, and perhaps to the twittering 'lark' and the 'fine and fair' morning. The humming accompaniment allows the solo tune to soar untrammelled but adds, by way of its sensuous harmony, a whiff of nostalgia for the Old England that, in 1905, was already on the way out. Despite the increasing density of the harmonies—which intermittently change the mode from Dorian to Aeolian—all the parts *sing* in Grainger's harmonic polyphony or polyphonized harmony. A technique that in the dances is light and lucid here becomes, in association with such lyrical lines and heartfelt poetry, pathetic and potentially tragic.

In the third stanza the chorus, expanded from four to five parts, underlines this tragic potential with intenser chromaticism. At the end of the verse the chorus takes over from the tenor soloist, now singing the words of the next stanza in radiant resonance. While they tell us that if meeting is a pleasure, parting is a pain, the soloist wails a chromatic obbligato, descending from a high A flat, as though weeping for the pity of it and for the sorrow of the world (see Example 14). The chorus take over the tenor's drooping chromatics to lead into the final stanza, in which the young man vows undying constancy, albeit with tremulous melismata on the keywords 'die' and 'loves'. The folk-poem itself, being about the precarious possibility of human love and the inevitability of death, is at once particular and universal. Grainger's 'Brigg Fair' is a perfect piece that can never grow old—unlike the young lovers, and you, and I.

In 1907 Grainger presented the tune in his arrangement to Frederick Delius, remarking that in Delius and himself 'many of the same impressions must have occurred in somewhat the same proportions to produce moments of *indistinguishable likeness*'. Delius concurred, and in the same year created his wondrous 'orchestral rhapsody', calling on Percy's arrangement as well as the tune itself. Some years later, the story runs, the aged Joseph Taylor was taken to the Queen's Hall to hear Beecham conduct

Example 14 'Brigg Fair', pp. 4–5.

Example 14 *cont.*

hum with closed mouths

hum with closed mouths

hum with closed mouths *ff*

hum with closed mouths

*soften lots*

*soften bit by bit*

(tog.)

*mp*   *soften*

*f*

*soften*

hum with closed mouths

Delius's *Brigg Fair*. When 'his' tune rang out after the preludial doodlings, Joseph, rising to his feet, sang along with the orchestra. The incident must have caused some consternation among the audience, not to mention the concert-hall attendants. Even if the story is apocryphal, it ought to be true and has the truth of allegory, since through Grainger's and Delius's advocacy the Folk were meeting folk, namely us.

Hardly less beautiful than the tenor-and-chorus 'Brigg Fair' is the wordless choral setting of the 'Irish tune from County Derry' that Percy discovered, not 'live', but in Petrie's published collection, where there are no words to it, though several ditties—the most familiar being 'Danny Boy'—have been appended. The melody has become a household word through a memorability perhaps attributable to the fact that it is closer than most folk-songs—though Grainger says it is 'undoubtedly very old'—to what people trained on harmonic and tonal music think of as a good tune. Not only is the melody unambiguously Ionian or diatonic major; it is also clearly structured in balanced antithetical phrases, with a beginning, middle, and end. This seems to imply modulation, and even a harmonic substructure to the tune itself; certainly the ear, having heard it harmonized so many times, tends subconsciously to supply the harmony latent in, though absent from, the monophonic tune. It may even be a rare example of a folk-song that sounds better—not merely different or, unless arranged by a Grainger, all too often worse—harmonized than in purely linear form.

In any case Grainger's several versions, which must have played a part in the tune's widespread popularity, are unrivalled: whether in the original wordless choral setting of 1902, in the dishing-up for piano of 1911, or in the later arrangements for string orchestra, wind-band, and symphony orchestra (the last for the Stokowski recording of 1952). The vocal version remains the most affecting—predictably, given Grainger's habit of arranging folksongs by adding other 'tone-strands' that, even in a homophonic texture, themselves resemble folk melodies. In the 1902 version the tune and the added tone-strands dovetail in a new entity that never effaces the monodic melody, however mysteriously the voices cross and recross. In a magical reconciliation of Delius with Bach the inner parts always sing—as for that matter do Delius's in the extreme chromaticism of the scalp-prickling wordless chorus in *A Song of the High Hills*. The secret may lie in what

Delius called 'the sense of flow', whereby something like Bach's 'long flow form' arouses exaltation instead of what might have been sentimentality. Interestingly enough, Grainger manages to create a similar effect in the solo-piano version; as in 'The Sussex Mummers' Christmas Carol', the piano spacing effects an illusion of choral homogeneity wherein harmony is a product of interdependent voices. The air is at once an individual and a corporate act. Though the music sounds folkily spontaneous, Grainger couldn't have achieved this had not instinct been abetted by his impeccable (Bach-based) technique.

Many of the old country singers, Grainger pointed out,

retain the freshness of their voices until such advanced ages as seventy years or more when they still enjoy a command of certain phases of technique which even our greatest art singers might try (as they certainly will not do) in vain to imitate, notably an enormous range of staccato and pianissimo effects. They seldom aim at attempting anything resembling a genuine legato style, but use their breath more as do some birds and animals, in short stabs and gushes of quickly contrasted twittering, pattering and coughing sounds which (to my ears at least) are as beautiful as they are amusing. Somewhat similar non-legato tendencies may be noticed in the fiddling of British and Scandinavian peasants, who are as fond of twiddles and quirks as are the old singers, and do not try to exchange the 'up and down' physical nature of the bow for the attainment of the continuous tone.

Rhythmic irregularities or distortions of pitch in a melody are not mistakes occurring in a predetermined pattern, but are part of folk music's complexity, which is different from, though not less developed than, our own. The very lack of our kind of harmonic consciousness makes possible their kinds of linear and rhythmic consciousness; and can help us, if we will allow it to, to revise our crude notions of what in-tuneness means.

Grainger's most thorough discussion of these matters is in his article on 'Collecting with the Phonograph', published in the *Journal* of the Folksong Society for May 1908. He points out how all his Lincolnshire singers regarded the tunes they sang as inseparable from the words; in narrative ballads with multiple stanzas the musical variants between the verses were always a consequence of the words and, however often they were performed, remained consistent with each particular stanza. Some singers preserved a fairly regular pulse, others favoured extreme irregularities in a given song. Folk performance was highly 'artistic', though its values were not those of orthodox art music. What applies to rhythm applies complementarily to pitch and modality. Gradually, Grainger came to the conclusion that although one may roughly call the modes his singers used Ionian, Aeolian, Dorian, and Mixolydian, they virtually never sang 'in' a particular mode. Both sixths and sevenths wavered between major and minor, as did thirds; sevenths that are sung flat in the upper octave, may be sharp in the lower; and sharp or sharpish sevenths may be introduced as passing, or even gliding, notes. Grainger's conclusion is that 'singers do not seem to have sung in different and distinct modes but to have rendered their modal songs in one single loosely knit modal scale, embracing within itself the combined mixolydian, dorian, and aeolian characteristics'. This is only what one would expect of an instinctual art, though categorizing scholars seemed reluctant to accept it—at least until computerized evidence made it 'scientifically' irrefutable. But Grainger came to these conclusions decades before ethnomusicology became a quasi-scientific discipline: so it is worth-while to compare Grainger's transcriptions of two versions of the same song, 'Lord Bateman', as uttered by the sweetly lyrical Joseph Taylor, and the erratic George Wray, whose variants between stanzas are indeed startling. (The two versions may be found in Teresa Balough's *Selected Writings by and about Percy Grainger*.) Grainger's transcriptions also afford insight into folk ornamentation ('twiddles and arabesques'), which are always boldly attacked and, far from being 'the quaverings of old and shaky voices, are introduced to give point and flourish'. Dynamics are also meticulously notated, demonstrating how any sforzando or whispery effect always had expressive point in relation to the basic mezzo piano—which most singers sensibly favoured, since they expected to keep going over long periods of time.

Grainger also discusses the manifestations of 'variable modality' in some instrumental music, especially Shetland fiddle-tunes in which a neutral pitch, flexibly arbitrating between sharp and flat thirds, sixths, and sevenths, seemed to be habitual. Cultivated art may have its autonomy, but it is not absolute, and art music may degenerate into 'frozen inspiration'. As Grainger puts it, 'the spectacle of one composer producing music for thousands of drones (totally uncreative themselves, and hence totally out of touch with the phenomenon of artistic creation) will no longer seem normal or desirable, and then the present gulf between the mentality of composers and performers will be bridged'. Although the literate musical instruction of the conservatories at this date cannot and should not be displaced, Grainger is on the mark in stressing that there are other basic aspects of musical technique that can be acquired only 'in the reiterated physical actions of rowing, marching, leaping, dancing, cradle-rocking etc., that called work-songs, dance music, ballads and lullabies into life'. As Grainger put it, 'uncivilized lives abound in music, and primitive modes of living, however terrible some of them may appear to educated and refined people, are seldom so barren of "mental leisure" as the bulk of our civilized careers'. Whereas in modern society, art encroaches on life, in so-called primitive societies life encroaches on art. H. G. Wells, accompanying Percy on a folk-song hunt in Gloucestershire, observed that Grainger noted down not merely 'the music and the dialect of the songs, but also many characteristic scraps of banter that passed between the old agriculturists'. When he remarked that Percy seemed to be notating not merely songs, but also a way of life, the musician retorted that there was no distinction. 'Primitive music is too complex for untrained ears', or at least for ears trained to listen for the wrong thing. The artistry of his untrained singers was, on its own terms, consummate. Each knew what he or she was after, and refashioned traditional material by way of 'the impress of personality on unwritten music'. Grainger recounts how he played to one of his singers a phonograph recording of the same tune sung by another performer, expressing the opinion that it was 'very fine'. To this the old man retorted: 'I don't know about *fine*; all I know is, it's *wrong*.' In his dishings-up of traditional songs Grainger claimed only to be giving his own interpretation, as did a genuine folk-singer, except that, being a modern man and conservatory-trained musician, he used more than purely melodic-rhythmic resources.

When he was a student at Frankfurt Grainger was encouraged to enter for the prestigious Mendelssohn Prize. He asked his tutors whether, should he win, he could use the money to study Chinese music in China: to which the reply was, 'We don't give prizes to idiots.' The notion of World Music, and the approaches to Unwritten Music mentioned above, are now commonplaces. But Grainger had arrived there before 1910, and all the remarks quoted above had been published in the Folksong Society *Journal* of 1908, as already mentioned, or in an article in *The Musical Quarterly* for July 1915. We have frequently observed how

Grainger's settings show respect for the original conditions of performance, whether in dance-hall (*Strathspey and Reel*), or village chapel ('The Sussex Mummers' Christmas Carol') or on a lonely rural hill ('Brigg Fair'). This aggressively personable young man taught the virtue of humility: as is most evident in the body of music wherein he is not so much transcribing or arranging folk material as effecting its ritual re-enactment. In the next chapter we will consider a selection of such pieces.

# 5

## GRAINGER'S GUISING
### *Music as Ritual Action and Magic Spell*

The boundary between an arrangement of a folk-song or a re-creation of it is, of course, hard to define. Grainger always brought a re-creative imagination to bear on traditional material; even when he was notating a song in quasi-scientific spirit, reproducing the exact effects of a given performance, he was engaged in a 'making' as contrasted with an ironed-out transcription served up for use in schools and colleges. For this reason even a very short transcription may be a fantasy, if not a meander. A case in point is the exquisite setting of 'The Sprig of Thyme', as sung to Grainger by Joseph Taylor and sketched out in 1907, though not formally dished up for voice and piano until 1920, as a 'loving birthday gift' for his mother. Grainger notates it in the Ionian mode on A, traditionally a key of youth and innocence, and transcribes Taylor's singing precisely, preserving both the poetry of his Lincolnshire dialect, and the spontaneous linear ornamentation and rhythmic irregularities with which he graced the tune. A modern singer, if of good will, could sing this Grainger-notated vocal part unaccompanied, producing something not altogether remote from Taylor's original. The piano part, on the other hand, is pure Grainger in his Delian vein, except that it is marvellously written for an instrument that Delius wasn't partial to or clever with. Especially interesting is the fact that Grainger's pianistic sophistication takes cues from Taylor's improvised rhythms and ornaments, such as the Scotch snaps and mordent-like twiddles. The piano sonorities and the fluid modulations are so luminously disposed on the keyboard that they too convey a '*premier matin du monde*' flavour in tune with the tune. The folk poetry and the folk-song, poised between love and death, mate the promise of young love to the inexorability of time and thyme (see Example 15).

Though this setting would have fitted into the previous chapter well enough, it hints at a 'magic' quality more patent in another song directly about the relation between love and death.

Example 15  'The Sprig of Thyme', high voice version, ending.

The setting of 'Died for love' was made in 1906 for a female voice with piano or a wind trio of flute, clarinet, and bassoon. When Grainger turned it into a solo piano piece he did not merely dish up a tune, but rather evoked a scene and a small drama. The tune sings in middle register, as sadly and sweetly as if the basically percussive piano had been metamorphosed into the young woman who has died, or is dying, for love, while undulating figurations (derived from the original wind trio) twine around her like babbling birds. Although the piece lasts only one minute, it encompasses a life and a mode of living; and although Grainger didn't invent the tune, his genius induces its rebirth. A quotation from the piece's end (in Grainger's manuscript) reveals how Bach-like the polyphonic texture is, despite the quasi-impressionistic sound (see Example 16).

Example 16 'Died for Love', piano solo, ending.

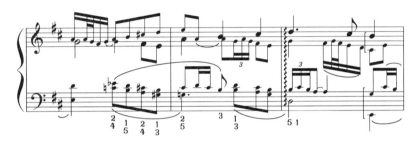

Another minute piece of unexpected poignancy is the setting of 'One more day, my John'—a sea-shanty arranged as 'Death Song for Hjalman Thuren' and dished up for piano in 1915. Grainger's note informs us that the song was traditionally sung at sea, the day before making the home port. 'Such a ditty is a late survival of "music of superstition", that is: music employed as a spell to propitiate the hostile, malign or insuperable forces of nature—oceans, rivers, storms and the like.' Since the piece is not an action-song like a sea-shanty proper, but rather a magic spell securing return to the safety of home, it is not surprising that it charms us in more than one sense, and is set in Grainger's magic-nostalgic key of F sharp major. Nothing could be more distant from the scarifying music of 'oceans, rivers, storms and the like' which we will soon encounter in Grainger's most famous sea-shanty setting, 'Shallow Brown'.

The border between an arrangement and a meander begins to be crossed in 'The Merry King', a tune arranged for mixed chorus in 1905–6. Much later, in 1936–9, Percy dished it up for piano, making a substantial work lasting four-and-a-half minutes. There are no formal complexities, for Grainger simply repeats the tune, taken down from the singing of Alfred Hunt of Wimbledon, four times, with a slight pause between each stanza. What results might be called a meander in that each statement grows more richly fanciful: plain diatonicism turns into a flowing texture ripe with dissonant suspensions, and then into chromaticism with interior polyphonies as luxuriant as those of Delius himself. Grainger meanders from his source in that he hears it with increasingly intense consciousness and retrospection. Even more remarkable in this vein is the second version of 'The Hunter in his Career', a song set in 1904 for double men's chorus and two pianos. This choral piece, lasting a mere minute-and-a-half, was transformed in 1928 into a virtuoso piano piece lasting more than twice as long, for a Grainger-like pianist of exceptional physicality and alacrity. The virtuosity is so physical in effect that it makes us want to career across the room—much as Percy, after a recital, released adrenalin by charging around a concert hall, hopefully making it back to the podium before the applause had subsided. (One version of this legend claims that Percy executed this whirlwind peregrination during the orchestral tutti preceding his playing of the cadenza in the first movement of the Grieg Piano Concerto!)

In the piano version of 'The Hunter in his Career' 'art' takes slight precedence over folk music. More commonly, Grainger's rambles around folk tunes, being ritual activity or magic spell, transfer the village green to wherever the performance is happening. In play-songs, work-songs, and narrative ballads combining instruments with voices, the effect is not to make the settings more 'arty'; on the contrary, they become more immediate, especially when (as was often the case) the vivacious composer was himself at the piano. The finest tribute one can pay to Grainger's folk-music settings is to recognize that they provide substitutes for, though not equivalents to, the 'careless rapture' of folk performance.

This works at a variety of levels. A light and slight example is a game-song, 'There was a pig went out to dig', modestly set in 1905 for women's voices unaccompanied. The piece tickles the fancy with its ingenuity but doesn't so sophisticate the game that real folk wouldn't laugh at it. Grainger's success as a setter of folk-songs is related to the fact that he is never arch—as in this capacity a much greater composer and no less 'natural' talent, Benjamin Britten, occasionally is. A comparably playful game-song is 'Six dukes went afishing', a gentle but fetching tune set for mixed chorus in 1905, but expanded in a longer, passacaglia-like version with flute, between 1905 and 1910. Still more elaborate in conception is 'I'm seventeen come Sunday', which was again collected in the vintage year of 1905 and dished up in 1912 for mixed chorus and brass, or strings, or piano, or compromises between all three. This dance-song begins with voices in unaccompanied unison, then in vigorous homophony, then with brass accompaniment and optional piano and percussion, as the verse tell the tale. The polyphonic scoring for brass stirs the guts, reanimating the virility of a legendary village band, with a technical virtuosity that can sound like a chuckle or chortle. Once more, art and life prove, for Grainger, inseparable.

'Bold William Taylor', though comical, can hardly be characterized as 'light'. Scored in 1908 for mezzo-soprano solo and an elastic room-music group it tells a violent story in which a woman, disguised as a man, pursues and shoots her faithless lover. The woman is not personalized—the part is often sung by a baritone— and the song's deadpan humour does not disguise, though it defuses, our savager impulses. Words and tune are presented straight but rough, while the band's rhythmic underlay impartially embraces the fire and farce of the text. Occasional snatches of chromatic harmony are ambiguous in effect—responsive to the woman's bold behaviour and perturbed state, yet more than a little comic. Physiological and psychological therapy is endemic to the action-music of the Folk.

'Lord Maxwell's Goodnight', dating from 1904, also tells a tragic tale but without ambiguity or irony. While the noble tune is sung straight, by solo tenor, the harmonization for four strings intensifies the melodic climax as, in each stanza, the tale grows grimmer. Action-therapy also typifies 'The Lost Lady Found', a narrative adventure-song, which was also a dance. Mrs Hill, who first sang it to Lucy Broadwood, acquired it from an old cook who danced as she sang, beating time with her iron pattens. A ballad was also a ballet, from the Italian *ballare*, to dance; and Grainger sets the sturdy Dorian tune in passacaglia-style, beginning with unison melody percussively accompanied. In his notes to the published version Grainger says that the chorus should mime, if not dance, the story, articulating the rhythms and cross-rhythms 'hammeringly', clearly, and 'very detached'. He appends specific dance-steps that go with the song, and recommends that they be borne in mind, if not acted out, by the performers. As the alarming story unfolds the instrumental backing grows more complex, though the line remains plainly modal. Interlacing ululations from wordless men's voices express fear lest the lost lady, stolen by three gypsies, may have been murdered, but her faithful lover, having sought her across the wide world, gets her home just in time to reprieve her uncle, unjustly accused of her murder, from the gallows. The unremittent beat and the imperviousness of the tune itself to accident or distress splendidly triumph; full chorus lends lustre to the final jubilation in fanfare-like la-laings through heroic fourths, fifths, and octaves.

Most of the numbers discussed in this chapter have been action-songs, hopefully with therapeutic effect, before being artistic communication. Grainger's finest music occurs, however, when folk tradition and personal communication become identified. Such a song is the setting of 'Willow, willow', originally made for solo voice, strings, and guitar in 1902; by 1911 there were also versions with more strings and piano or harp. The words are familiar through having been used by Shakespeare as Desdemona's death-song, and the melody itself, in the Aeolian mode on E but occasionally substituting the sharp for the flat sixth and seventh, may be of Elizabethan provenance; false relations between the major and minor third appear in the original tune as well as in Grainger's harmony. As does Shakespeare in his tragedy, Percy reveals the universal implications of the words' lament. The string lines—with solo viola echoing the piteous falling fifth at the beginning of the tune—engage in dialogue with the voice, while the plangent guitar or harp deputizes for a Renaissance lute. The guitar-lute grows more active in rising arpeggios as the stanzas unfold; in the last stanza the harmony is melancholicaly chromaticized and the quasi-seventeenth-century false relations pierce deeper (see Example 17).

If this song is not action, it is magic, its effect depending on its breaking the time-barrier. The threnody of the 'poor soul', sighing

Example 17   'Willow, willow', score, p.11.

Example 17 *cont.*

by the proverbially weeping willow, is an age-old folk archetype; the Shakespearian association provides an Elizabethan context; while the frail strands of melody and the gently chromatic harmony bring our twentieth-century regret, whether it be for a lost way of life or simply for the grief inherent in living, loving, and dying. Complementary to this is 'Shallow Brown', which is as violent as 'Willow, willow' is gentle. For this sea-shanty comes across as an extraordinarily dramatic, even melodramatic, song of personal loss, as well as a communal action-song: which was collected in 1908 from John Perrin, 'a remarkably gifted deep-sea sailor songster', and set in 1910 for solo voice or unison chorus with a male chorus and an orchestra of thirteen (or more) instruments. Versions were also made for unison chorus or solo voice with piano. Although the piece is always performed by men, John Perrin told Grainger that the song was supposed to be sung by a woman standing on the quay, addressing Shallow Brown as his ship weighed anchor. Nobody knows why he was called Shallow, unless it be in reference to his feckless nature.

But although a woman's voice would make better sense of the story, the song is of course a sea-shanty, a genre from which women were *ipso facto* excluded. In a letter of 1907 Grainger wrote of the communal intensity of sea-shanties, which banded together roughly sensual men as they traversed the high seas, racked by their individual as well as communal fears and frenzies:

These poor bodily-strong devils living in the unnatural shipboard round, with minds engrossed in nought but money, food, drink and sex, but having little of any of these things, yearned aloud for them in their songs. Naturally, wholly cut off from women's atmosphere as they were, their view [of sex] is rank & mean & lacking in all vestiges of tenderness; but just because of all this, because it is so solely the UNREDEEMED MALE ANIMAL'S UTTERANCE, it has distinction.

This comes over even in Grainger's brief version of the well-known 'Shenandoah', dating from 1907; in 'Shallow Brown' frenzy attains an edge that suggests personal involvement. A desperately as well as joyously physical man, Grainger confessed in a letter written in 1910 to his lover Karen Holten:

I am incapable of real sympathy, because real suffering is with-suffering, and I am incapable of suffering. Therefore I am not ever really unkind. Pain, to myself or others, is a thing I instinctively fight tooth and nail . . . I can join in all mirth with anyone, but I can sorrow with none, not even myself . . . The very scenery that stirs me and that I love is lifeless and unproductive, useless and unkind to man—Australian deserts, lifeless and unproductive, useless and unkind Highlands, the SEA. Only the aftermath in the life struggle (the time for play, the lives that can be thrown away, the country that can be let go waste) delights me. None of the birthful, needed, earnest-rooted things . . . But I have my place in the scheme, alongside the whip, the spur, & the cold morning British bath. My work, through my art, is to refresh, to round up stragglers and to hound up each and every one in the scrimmage. Not a very deep call (certainly not a dear one, maybe) but still clean & healthful &—& this is

my strength—a call that's not been properly sounded in music before . . .
War & sport & wild country & raw pride pick me up & *carry me away*
& *drunken me.*

There is a link between that extraordinary passage, which
obliquely involves Grainger's sado-masochistic proclivities, and
the impact made on us by his setting of 'Shallow Brown'. Also
pertinent is a passage from a letter written to Karen in the previous year, 1909: 'Sorrow is fine & productive for me. Fear of
death & loss, destruction & forgetfulness spur me to compose,
collect, preserve & embalm . . . There must be someone to sit
mourningly & to hold the cold hands of dead races, men and languages, lost battles & failed enterprises.' If these are odd words
to be uttered by a man usually thought of as the epitome of *brio*
and bounce, Grainger, a creature of contradictions, knew that his
extroversion hid an inner terror. In 'Shallow Brown' the lid is
off.

The grand tune rings out in Nordic raucousness, in Ionian B
flat major, but with savagely dislocated accents and contrasted
dynamics prompted by the desperation behind the words: 'O
Shaller Brown, you're goin ter leave me, Shaller Brown, don't
ne'er deceive me.' The notation of this vocal line, with its irregular triplets and microtonal slides, seems to be close to the notations taken down from John Perrin's singing, while the refrains of
the male chorus, snarling Shallow's name, sound comparably
authentic. Throughout, the piano's furious tremolandos or 'wog-
glings', intended to 'suggest wafting wind-borne surging sounds
heard at sea', underline the fluctuating dynamics with powerful,
sometimes fiercely dissonant harmonic shifts. The ambiguously
resolutory end—with woggling modulations through E flat and C
minor, and mysterious changes of gear between triads of D flat
major and D minor—deeply disturbs, until the sea-sounds fade on
an unresolved flat seventh (or blue note) of B flat (see Example
18). Such effects are scary enough in the version for baritone and
piano but become—especially in the climax with the screeching
clarinet in the previous stanza—horrendous in the full room-
music version, wherein wind parts plumb oceanic depths through
a babel of guitars, mandolins, and ukuleles, thrumming madly in
support of the inexorable piano. Grainger is said to have played
this piano part swaying in a semi-conscious state, indeed 'carried
away and drunkened'. There is no more alarming instance of this

Example 18 'Shallow Brown', ending, voice and piano.

particular Percy-paradox, whereby music traditionally communal becomes a personal testament.

In 'Shallow Brown', a sea-shanty evoking the wild ocean and the desperation of human loss, Grainger approaches whirlwinds of feeling beyond British agrarian rurality. So we may use the number as a transition to a body of his work as yet undiscussed: that

87

associated with the Nordic myths and sagas which, at his mother's instigation, had dominated his boyhood. His settings of tunes from the Faroe Islands are literally transitional since—as Grainger put it in a programme note:

The Faroe Islands lie between the Shetland Islands and Iceland, and the Faroe Islanders are descendents of those Norwegian sea-rovers who, in the 9th century, settled the lands 'west over sea'. The Islanders are famous for their good looks, their highly becoming national costumes, their daring as cliff-scaling egg-gatherers, and their passion for dancing. The language is closely akin to Icelandic (Old Norse) and folksongs of many periods abound in the islands. Until recently no musical instruments (not even organs and harmoniums in churches) were known on the Faroes. So the music accompanying the dance was narrative dance-folksongs—dance tunes sung by voices instead of played on instruments. Long rimed stories about legendary and historical figures and groups—the Volsungs, the Nibelungs, Siegfried (Sjurdar), Charlemagne, Roland, Attila, Tristram, Nornagest etc.,—as well as versified excerpts from Icelandic sagas were chanted by a single voice (foresinger) answered by symbolically significant refrains sung by a chorus in unison, without harmonies of any kind.

Since Faroe Island folk-songs are also dances, they have preserved their clear-cut rhythmic shapes, in direct association with bodily movement. The dancing and singing habits of the people tend to be orgiastic, generating—according to Percy—'group frenzy of a religious, erotic or war-like character'. He found here surviving evidence of the kind of life-and-music he proleptically envisaged in *The Warriors*; when he has the real thing to fire him, he produces finer, and also more original, music. 'Let's dance gay in green meadow' was taken down in the field, and sketched out for chorus in 1905, but was then laid aside until, in 1932, it was 'worked out'—for three players on one harmonium! In 1943 Grainger rehashed this for the more normal four hands on two pianos: in which form it was deservedly championed by Benjamin Britten, and has achieved a measure of celebrity. The tune, deriving from the metrics of Icelandic folk verse, is consistently in seven-bar phrases, which sometimes overlap. Irregularity enhances vivacity, as the tune, beginning pentatonically, embraces a heptatonic scale on A that might be called Phrygian with the sixth and seventh ambiguously minor or major. Grainger's scoring is light and luminous; the form is incrementally repetitive, with extensions to and contractions of the initial melodic seed. The harmonies grow sharply dissonant and briefly chromatic, but always function as a quasi-percussive accompaniment to capering feet; the registration may be grumpily low or glitteringly high on the keyboard. In such body-music there cannot be even momentary changes in tempo. Grainger says, in his programme note, that he has tried to capture the 'tireless keeping-onness' of the Faroe Island narrative songs, which may run to two hundred or more verses. His settings are not variations in the conventional sense which implies clearly defined beginnings and endings in sectional forms. On the contrary, 'my dance-folksong settings aim at giving an impression of large-size continuity and unbroken form-flow— with willingness on my part to welcome whatever monotony may result from this method'. For a long time jazz-variation techniques have worked on this principle, while Grainger offers a more specific harbinger of minimalism and of today's urban pop, which aims to negate temporal progression, growth, change, and consummation, in order to create a continuum within which we momentarily live. Both jazz and urban pop have often sought 'group frenzy of a religious, erotic or war-like character', and both have used the device of the fade-out to suggest a mesmeric 'keeping-onness' that in some cases becomes tiresome rather than tireless. Grainger may be tireless, but tiresome he is not, for his 'long flow form' here validates the affinities he'd found between Icelandic dance-song and Bach. Certainly, this piece refreshes jaded bodies and spirits, leaving us, like the redoubtable Faroese, ready for more. The ambiguity of the modality contributes to this wideawake feeling: for although the nodal point of the tune is A, overlapping cadences veer between A and C, and the last clause simply stops, without conclusion, on a C major triad (see Example 19).

A similar tonal oddity typifies another Faroe dance-setting, also taken down in the field in 1905, but not worked out until 1931. Although 'The Rival Brothers' tells a fierce tale of jealousy and was originally scored for chorus and an instrumental ensemble, it found definitive form as a wordless piano piece for two or four hands on one piano. The tune is perky, built on a rising arpeggio incorporating a dotted rhythm. The tonality starts as Ionian F major, but the stark four-part harmony teeters between triads of F major, A minor, and G minor, none being a palpable tonic. Triplet cross-rhythms within the duple time animate repeats of

Example 19 'Let's dance gay in green meadow', two-piano version, ending.

the tune, while the bass line grows increasingly physical or, in Grainger's word, 'jumpy'. Momentum is further encouraged by chromatic inner parts that give extra bite to the cross-rhythms. Yet the dance goes nowhere, except in a round. Action-music lasts only as long as the action; and again, the piece simply stops, on a chord of G minor.

Two of Grainger's Faroe Island pieces directly emulate the ritualism of their models. 'Father and Daughter', written in 1908–9, is scored for five solo voices, described as 'narrators' because they tell the tale, with a double mixed chorus actively representing the 'tribe', and with three orchestral groups of brass, strings, and mixed mandolins and guitars (as many as possible). The tune is in fast duple time, in F major tending to pentatonicism; many repeated notes emphasize the dance's physicality, but drama is generated by the thrilling antiphony between the choral groups and the soloists. The instrumental groups enter incrementally, enhancing the orgiastic abandon in the process. The end, when the 'massed' guitars and mandolins have entered in fullest pelt, is sensational, and one is not surprised when John Bird tells us that, at the performance at the Queen's Hall in 1912, Grainger received twelve curtain-calls, and the piece had to be repeated twice. Perhaps it isn't fortuitous that the tale that called forth so much Graingerish exuberance is violent: a father savagely murders his daughter's lover and in retribution is burnt in his house by the girl.

A companion to this stirring piece is 'The Merry Wedding', which uses no real folk-tunes, though it was inspired by verses from the same collection, Hammershaimb's 'wonderful Faroesk Anthology' of 1886. There is no place in this wedding-dance for the 'blood, violence and disaster' typical of 'Father and Daughter', but plenty of scope for energy and vivacity. The words' swinging couplets are set for nine solo voices, chorus, piano, and strings. Percy's original tune, in E flat major, begins with an upward bouncing arpeggio and a buoyant dominant modulation, and prances in consistent dotted rhythm throughout the dance. Scrunchy suspensions and passing dissonances give the music sinew appropriate to a wild landscape, but without threatening the sweet lyricism or the tenderness of the words ('Brown is my silky hair, snow-white is my skin so fair'). As the couplets build up incrementally, the music gathers excitement by way of fleetingly chromatic inner parts, of bitonality and bimodality, and of cross-rhythms of two against the prevailing three. Solos, half-chorus, and full chorus interweave in the onward momentum, though the sense of anchorage in heroic E flat major is unbroken. This generous overflow of Grainger's vivacity of body and spirit must have pleased the dedicatee, Percy's *kammerat*, Karen Holten, as it does us.

We've noted that Grainger's inspiration sprang mostly from his youth and that his music did not 'develop', either within individual compositions or throughout his career. But one might make out a case that his Faroe Island works grow in sophistication, and that the same happens in his closely related 'Danish' pieces. Grainger had first visited Denmark in 1905, his Lincolnshire *annus mirabilis*, on a concert tour with his cellist friend Herman Sandby. While in Denmark he met the folk-song collector Hjalmar Thuren, whom he found highly congenial. Thuren died in 1912; but in the next year Grainger met the illustrious folk-song scholar Evald Tang Kristensen, now in his eighties, but revered by Percy as the epitome of all a collector ought to be. Partly because of Rose's nervous disorders, and partly because of the outbreak of war, Grainger was not able to visit Denmark again until after his mother's death in 1922. Then, a folk-song collecting trip to Jutland was just what Percy needed to assist his recuperation. Now equipped with a phonograph as well as his lively ears, and inspired by Kristensen's example, Percy made his own collection of Danish songs between 1922 and 1927. From it he created a major work which he called *Danish Folksong Suite*: wherein the tunes are treated in a rather grand manner befitting their Nordic heroism. Although the scoring is very elastic—ranging from four single string or wind instruments to string orchestra with piano and harmonium and so to a version for large orchestra with important parts for piano, organ, and marimba—Percy regarded this as preferably a 'big' work for large forces, which he handled with expertise. The chromaticism of the textures, with the harmonium 'tremolando possibile', is as extreme as that of *The Power of Rome*, but here the strength of the melodies justifies the luxuriance.

The first number, 'The Power of Love' (very distinct from that of Rome!) recounts a fierce tale of a young man who murders one of his girl's seven brothers, a fact which she—such is the power of love—accepts as all in the day's work or play. Though we don't hear the words in this orchestral suite, the passion comes across in an orchestral rhapsody almost worthy of Delius. An autobiographical factor probably bears on this, for Grainger tells us that this was the first music he had written since Rose's suicide in 1922. The song had been 'grippingly, piercingly, heart-searchingly' sung for him by a Mrs Anne Nielsen Post, 'a wondrously gifted folksinger of the very finest type, whose Nordic comeliness, knee-slapping mirth and warm-heartedness, paired with a certain inborn aristocratic holding-back of herself, reminded me of my mother'. Unsurprisingly, he put into his setting 'my new-born awareness of the doom-fraught undertow that lurks in all deep love'. Mother Rose is also evoked in the second number, 'Lord Peter's Stableboy', but this time in happy memory since this was one of the verses from Kristensen's great anthology that Percy and Rose had often chanted to one another. Hearing the rousing seven-bar-phrased tune sung in 'manly, ringing tones' by Michael Poulsen, Percy set it as 'a tone-likeness of my mother's nature—sturdy, free, merry, peg-away, farm-like'. Percy's music fits that description exactly, generating bounce from the free-ranging polyphony, this time owing more to Bach than to Delius. Passing dissonances are scrunchy, but tonality is grandly 'open' as the main statements of the tune range from diatonic G major to E major to A major and thence to F sharp minor, with gentler, seductively chromatic episodes linking the rondo-like statements of the main tune. This apparently arbitrary key-sequence is appropriate to action-music for dancers who are not engaged in a Beethovenian spiritual pilgrimage hopefully struggling from A to Z. The dancing—as we've observed in other works—goes round and round, and where it stops is immaterial. Maybe there is in this case intuitive point in the fact that it stops, after all those clear major keys, in F sharp minor, in tribute to the down-to-earth sturdiness of Rose's nature, if not to her suicidal propensities.

The unsung words of this song are a disguise-ballad wherein a young woman (as in Grainger's favourite 'Bold William Taylor') dresses up as a man in order to pursue her lover. The words of 'The Nightingale', which for the third movement Grainger links with 'The Two Sisters', also recount a success story, though in a mood of open-eyed wonderment. For the carolling nightingale is really a girl bewitched by a proverbially wicked stepmother, but rescued by a noble knight. 'The Two Sisters', a tune of Scottish ancestry, seemed a suitable companion to 'The Nightingale' since it tells how a Good (blonde) Sister is murdered by a Bad (brunette) Sister out of jealousy; but Right triumphs over Wrong through the agency of two fiddling musicians. The tune, in a flowing triplet rhythm with aspiring sixth followed by a drooping scale, is of ineffable loveliness, and Grainger's harmonization and scoring are worthy of it. A solo violin and two solo cellos are used to ravishing effect, emerging from oily choirs of saxophones—favoured by Percy because of their human expressivity—and from tremulous organ and shimmering piano and harps. The ecstatic denouement of the story prompts modulation from the initial 'benedictory' G major to 'heavenly' E major, in which key the piece ends, albeit in a haze of added notes and with reverberating gong-tones on low piano strings, struck with a 'medium hard marimba mallet'. Again, the acuteness of Grainger's ear serves the fairy-tale magic of his poetic and dramatic themes.

The fourth movement is the longest, being a medley that links four tunes from Jutland. The chain makes cumulatively exciting sense, beginning with a bride-choosing song in which a young man opts for light and truth rather than wealth. Unsurprisingly, it's an open-hearted, simple-minded diatonic march in B flat major, with fanfare-like triads and thrusting dotted rhythms, scored with Grainger's typical polyphonic zest and rhythmic zip for full orchestra. Scrunchy chromatics and exhilarating cross-rhythms create an unbuttoned animation resembling Ives in his parade-band manner. The second tune, 'The Dragoon's Farewell', is supposed to be sung by a soldier setting out for the wars, but embraces retrospective sentiment rather than extrovert belligerence. The key, yanked up to B major if not quite as far as Grainger's glittering F sharp major, hints at a potential transcendence, and the pulse changes from a brisk march to a slowish triple beat. The tune, opening with a rising fourth, has affinities with the bride-choosing song but is more heartfelt because the young man faces dangers unknown.

This may be why the third movement brings in spiritual associations, for Grainger describes 'The Shoemaker from Jerusalem' as 'a very archaic religious song'. This tune also begins with a rising fourth, proceeding in a moderate 6/8 gait, in the Aeolian mode. The harmonization, however, grows sumptuously chromatic, instinct with loss and longing rather than with domestic pieties. But the everyday world takes over again in the last link in the chain, for this is a 'quarrelling song' bitonally introduced by triadic fanfares appropriately in false relation, but bounding into another triadic tune in E flat major and a blithe 3/8. Wildly chromatic part-writing soon pervades a clever contrapuntal interweaving of several of the medley's themes, making for a 'quarrel' that is apposite to the unheard words while also making a thrilling (Ivesian) climax to the suite (see Example 20).

Throughout, the orchestration of the *Danish Suite* is remarkably imaginative and skilful; and it is interesting that in the published

Example 20   'Jutish Medley', p. 35 of full score.

95

score of this particular work Grainger includes an essay on Elastic Scoring, addressed to potential conductors. He explains that he favours Elastic Scoring for the obvious reason that he wants his music to be performable in as many varied contexts as possible; but also to encourage musicians to experiment with the plethora of instruments now available, especially easy-to-play instruments like saxophone, harmonium, celesta, dulcitone, xylophone, marimba, guitar, banjo, ukulele, and sundry kinds of bells. All these instruments have a field-day in 'Jutish Medley'; and Grainger insists that experiment with all kinds of keyboard, percussion, and 'tuneful percussion', with choirs of saxophones and with unorthodox dispositions of string forces should be undertaken, if not by hopelessly hardened professional orchestras, then by music students in schools and colleges. This dethronement, or emancipation, of the conventional symphony orchestra accords with Grainger's belief that music today needs to involve participation between 'doers' rather than performance by a professional band before a captive audience. 'Let our orchestras grow naturally', he writes in his final paragraph; 'let us, in forming the orchestras of the present and the future, try using large numbers of the instruments that most abound today . . . If these instruments prove ineffective in massed usage, let us then discard such usage. But do not let us discard such usage without full trial.' In the years since Grainger wrote those words in 1929 this has to some degree happened, though the immense technical advance in the standards of youth orchestras has also meant that they compete with professionals on their own terms.

Grainger made a piano solo version of the 'Jutish Medley' around the same time as the orchestral version. It is one of his most impressive virtuoso works for solo piano, transferring to the keyboard much of the technical audacity evident in the orchestral work. The counterpointed melodies in the final 'quarrelling' section make considerable demands on the pianist, but prove equally rewarding to him and the listener, so brilliantly are they laid out on the keyboard. A piano version of 'The Nightingale and the Two Sisters', made much later in 1949, is among the most poignant of all Grainger's slow settings; Martin Jones, in his recording of the complete piano works, plays it ravishingly. Like so much of Delius, it is a quintessence of nostalgia that, far from enervating the senses, tingles them to fresh awareness. The secret, as with Delius himself, lies in the fact that the chromatic harmony is a tissue of individually audible melodic strands. Perhaps the intimacy of the piano version makes it even more heart-rending than the orchestral version. The spread chords hint at some bardic harp; and the magical coda loses nothing—at least under Martin Jones's hands—from the absence of warmly sustained orchestral brass. The piano texture glows.

Two of Grainger's late 'originals' may be mentioned here since, although they call on no traditional material Danish or otherwise, they have affinities with the slow rambles around Danish themes discussed above. Each is a bridal song, associated with one or the other of the two women who were, next to his mother, most important in his private life. 'A Bridal Lullaby' is a short piano piece written in 1916, as a wedding present for his one-time lover Karen Holten, in tender regret at what he had lost (partly through his mother's bloody-mindedness), but also in joy that Karen had found a more suitable if less exciting mate. It is a strangely touching little piece in Percy's bright-shining F sharp major, with sweetly piercing passing dissonances, chromatic harmony that is clinging but not cloying, and harp-style spread chords that recall the 'bardic' arpeggios in the piano setting of 'The Nightingale and the Two Sisters'. The music dissipates in 'woggling' added sixths, like cocktail-lounge jazz (see Example 21).

Example 21   'A Bridal, Lullaby', ending.

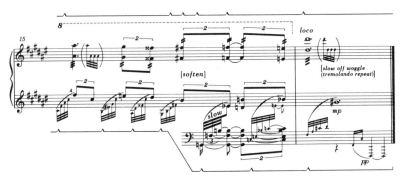

This idiom, sublimated, characterizes also the longer bridal piece dedicated 'To a Nordic Princess', which exists in versions for piano and for orchestra; mingling rapture with nostalgia in chromaticized harmonic polyphony it works best in its orchestral form. That it attains a passionate climax in mid-stream may be indicative of Percy's winning the Princess as his bride. She was Ella Ström, a Swedish girl whom he was able, his mother now dead, to woo and marry. He typically described her as

the perfect type of Nordic womanhood, half-boyish yet wholly womanly, whose soft flawless loveliness is like that of a fairy princess, whose wondrous radiance makes real for us the sun-goddesses of the nature-myths, whose broad shoulders, amazon limbs, fearless glances and freedom of deed and bearing recall the viking chieftesses of the sagas. Here is the bedrock aristocraticness of class, culture and breeding. To meet her is to have *all one's boyhood fairy-dreams and hero-dreams come true* (author's italics).

Poor Ella didn't let Percy down, though his song in her honour hardly lives up to his prescription. Finished in time for the wedding in the Hollywood Bowl in 1928, it sounds, in its opulent orchestral garb, more at home there than it would be at a Viking ritual feast. If Percy was in a sense growing up to accept the contingencies of life-as-it-is, rather than as it might have been or ought to be, he still makes better music when he acts out his dreams.

There is a similar rejection of play-acting in a new version of a work Grainger had composed in 1898, in the first flush of his Nordic fervour. *The Wraith of Odin* was originally a 'heroic' setting for two choirs and large orchestra of stanzas from a poem of Longfellow, telling of a ghostly visitation to a Nordic King's court. The ghost, who recounts to the company weird and wonderful tales of the natural and supernatural, turns out to be the god Odin, Norse version of one-eyed Wotan. In 1922, inspired by his folk-song collecting in Denmark, Grainger made a very different version of this early saga. Since it is scored for two pianos without voices, it cannot verbally tell the tale, and makes little attempt to re-create the drama of the original; instead, it becomes a psychologically subtle commentary on the effects of the fabled events on the assembled court. It has therefore something in common with Grainger's folk-song variations made around the same time, though its modal tune is original. It is far from being a major work, but that Grainger should modify his creations to meet the needs of the moment is credible and creditable. The play-acting of a Nordic saga no longer mattered, but to translate forgotten dreams into terms still psychologically relevant was another and better thing.

In this context we must mention another quasi-bardic ballad which, though of Scots rather than Danish origin, has bearing on Grainger's biography. *The Bride's Tragedy*, written in 1908–9 and scored in 1914 for two choirs and orchestras or piano, is conceived both as dramatic action and as ritual, with the small second chorus separated from the main chorus, sounding 'muffled and distant', as compared with the first chorus's ferocity. The words are a pretend-Scots ballad by Swinburne, whose grimly swinging rhythms and choric refrain effectively imitate the real thing. Here Swinburne—a *fin de siècle* poet who, like Grainger, was partial to flagellation—fuses the demotic and the mythic in a way parallel to the Kipling of the *Jungle Books* and *Barrack Room Ballads*, and Grainger creates for the words some heroically saga-like music. The first part, which is fast and ferocious, tells in free tonality and irregular rhythms of a young woman who, about to be married off to a man she abominates, is snatched away at the church porch by her true love. They ride off, pursued by the irate bridegroom, but are drowned in attempting to cross a turbulent river. The second part—perhaps it is better thought of as a coda—is no longer action-music but rather a dirge for the drowned lovers, in highly chromatic, wildly wandering polyphony, with weirdly echoing water noises and a fade-out in the 'distant' semi-chorus. Despite the rootless chromaticism, the final dolorous triad of C minor is death-laden.

Much later, in 1936, Percy wrote in a letter to his one-time lover Alfhild Sandby, that this *Bride's Tragedy* was

my personal protest against the sex-negation that our capitalistic world (assisted by mother, you, & by numberless other well-wishers) offered to young talents like me. A man cannot be a full artist unless he is manly, & a man cannot be manly unless his sex-life is selfishly brutal, wilful, unbridled. The situation called for a protest, & *The Bride's Tragedy* was my protest, & the angry chords on the brass (in the first singing of 'they lie dead and drownded') are my personal bitterness.

Although that transition from 'manliness' to 'brutality' is a characteristic *non sequitur*, it suggests why Percy was so obsessed with this work that he had it performed at the Evanston Festival, in commemoration of an anniversary of Rose's death. That he described the work as a requiem for her is a dubious tribute, given the theme; even so, the committed energy of the performance was such that Grainger received the 'greatest ovation' of his American career, at least up to that point. Love and hate were indeed entangled in paradoxical Percy, as were pleasure and pain.

It is worth noting that Percy was surprised, or affected to be surprised, that people found so much of his music 'merry and bright'. The entire musical world, he claimed, is 'oblivious of the whole world of bitterness, resentment, iconoclasm and denunciation that lies behind my music . . . I have always enjoyed composing. No "wretchedness" there. But the worth of my music will never be guessed, or its value to mankind felt, until the approach to my music is consciously undertaken as a "pilgrimage to sorrows".' These words were written in a letter to Michael Harrington dated 11 February 1941, but the attitude expressed was not new. For Grainger, even jolly dances like *Shepherd's Hey* were action-music which, against the odds, might serve to keep us going. They may have been play but were action rather than acting. His *Country Gardens* nurtured 'turnips rather than flowers', and 'my dance settings are energetic rather than gay—more like Russian than English music'. Although, as often, Percy exaggerates, he was on the mark in believing that his durability was inseparable from his toughness.

# 6

## OLD WORLDS FOR NEW

### *Rambling and Meandering through Four Mini-Masterpieces*

We have discovered that to categorize Grainger's works is difficult, if not impossible. Original compositions, transcriptions, arrangements, settings, and rambles or meanders cannot be codified, and Grainger's works always play havoc with time, and sometimes also with space. In this chapter we will consider four works which, however categorized, count as mini-masterpieces. Perhaps it is to the point that they tend to 'ramble' rather far from their sources in becoming Grainger's most enduring contribution to the 'heritage of music', independent of whatever significance one attributes to him in social history.

*My Robin is to the Greenwood Gone* was written in 1912 as an instrumental ramble around a popular song probably of Elizabethan provenance. The original scoring is for flute, cor anglais, and six strings, though Grainger later made versions for piano solo and for violin, cello, and piano. The piece is not a setting of a self-contained tune, in the manner of the Elizabethan virginalists' variation-sets on folk or popular tunes, including this one. For although the virginalists sometimes wrote long and texturally complex pieces on such melodies, they did not threaten the tune's identity. It was what it was, as part of folk tradition; as composers of some technical sophistication, they treated it in ways they found congenial and enlivening, but they did not challenge its autonomy. Grainger was not in their position, for the obvious reason that he lived three hundred years later. Even so, he had so lively an empathy with this song that he wanted to remake it; and that is precisely what he does, referring only to the first four bars of the tune, then rambling off on his own, returning to the fragment intermittently. The piece is indeed a rebirth, existing both in and out of time.

Separation from the tune's historical reality is suggested by Grainger's opening with a brief introduction in a swaying 6/8 pulse on the strings; the mode is Aeolian on E, with the sixth sometimes sharpened. The muted strings are lullaby-like in their rocking rhythm, and the fragments of the old song float or flutter on (unmuted) solo violin, and then on flute and cor anglais, as though emerging from sleep and dream. There's pathos in the answering phrase drooping *scalewise* through a sixth, then through the *interval* of a fifth. Tender chromatic passing-notes creep in as, from this 'once upon a time', bits of the tune come and go, ebb and flow, wax and wane, flower and fade—like the Robin of the title who, whether male or female, is both bird and beloved. The music breathes loss and regret, for Robin is gone; but it also burgeons with the wood's green promise, the tune swelling as the harmonies grow richer, then dissipating in Marvell's 'green thought in a green shade'. The structure, or non-structure, is accurately described as a ramble, though there is a vestigial da capo when—after plangent rising arpeggios on the lute-guitar and melancholic fragments on cor anglais entwined with strings—the original authentic snippet returns on flute. In the coda the tune vanishes over the hill, and maybe beyond the rainbow. Penetrative cor anglais is answered by a melismatically ornamented, antiquely Edenic flute, with string chords pizzicato and arco, recalling the lullaby-like introduction. They remain unresolved, on the borders of sleep, and fade out, off-key, on an F sharp major triad with an added 'blue' flat seventh. Since this seventh is an E it preserves awareness of the original tonic, although we are no longer 'in' it (see Example 22).

*My Robin* is a dream-piece and a miniature tone-poem and on both counts has affinities with Delius's shorter pastoral pieces. It differs from them, however, in that whereas Delius's nature-music—except possibly in the Grainger-inspired *Brigg Fair*—makes no reference to a specific time and place, Grainger's meander has precise origins in a tune and a past which, 'for the time being', is eternally present. This is another instance of how Grainger's music may be most original when most dependent on tradition.

Robin rambles in the greenwood for five-and-a-half minutes, a fair time for a single movement by Grainger. *Green Bushes*, described as a 'passacaglia on a folksong', lasts eight to nine minutes, which makes it a sizeable one-movement work. It was a direct product of the crucial year 1905/6, when Grainger garnered tunes in Lincolnshire; but in scoring this tune for small orchestra Percy knew that he was not making an arrangement, but was creating a com-position. In his introductory comments to the published score he explains the difference between a variation-set and a passacaglia. The former takes a tune as an entity and, in a sequence of variations, presents it in changing, even contrasted, lights: whereas a passacaglia is a dance-form evolved during the sixteenth and seventeenth centuries, and attaining consummation during the age of the classical Baroque. The dance itself was ceremonial, often associated with the marriage of very important persons. Musically, the form consisted of a ground bass in triple rhythm at moderate processional speed, repeated *ad libitum* as support to melodic parts that proliferate in cumulatively enhanced richness. Theoretically, the repetitions of the bass continue as long as the dancers need them. This might be determined by practical exigencies in so far as the dancers were often celebrants

Example 22 *My Robin is to the Greenwood Gone*, end, in score.

Example 22   *cont.*

who—a marriage being an occasion at once sacred and profane—
were called on to effect a ceremonial ingress or egress.

While a Renaissance or Baroque passacaglia was a sophisticated
concept appertaining to high life, it is obvious that the principle
involved is identical with that inherent in low-life ceremonies
such as a morris dance; as we noted, Grainger's *Shepherd's Hey*
functions like a passacaglia, though it isn't one. Interestingly
enough, Baroque composers often used folk or pop tunes as the
'ground' for their passacaglias or chaconnes, the two dance-forms
being barely distinguishable. Frescobaldi was especially partial to
the use of pop songs, such as the *Romanesca*, as ground-bass for a
passacaglia: perhaps the socially mighty liked to feel that they had
their feet on the earth, however high they held their noble heads.
The Elizabethan virginalists employed English pop tunes to similar ends, whether or not they used the term passacaglia to
describe their creations. In writing a 'passacaglia on a folksong',

Grainger was thus following a long-established precedent. Nor is the work unique in his *œuvre*, for we have noted that several of his folk-song settings follow the principle of varied repeats through a consistent pulse, if not necessarily over a basso ostinato. *Green Bushes* is distinguished from these other pieces mainly by its length, the unremittent nature of its beat, and the closely wrought consistency of its figurations. While Grainger opens traditionally with the tune in and as the bass, it soon pervades the whole texture. In one part or another it is always audible, proliferating into other related tunes, with ever-increasing polyphonic resource. Grainger never more powerfully emulated Bach's 'long flow form'; and was of course well aware that the greatest of all passacaglias is Bach's monumental organ work in C minor, for which the seed was nothing so memorable as a folk or pop tune, but literally a bass by a seventeenth-century organist, André Raison.

*Green Bushes* works so well because it is, for Grainger, the ideal extended form. Basically, it is corporeal action-music, like the simple *Shepherd's Hey*; and it does in more 'artistic' terms what is exuberantly achieved in 'Let's dance gay in green meadow', which we saw to be in effect a passacaglia that creates a continuum within which we 'live, move and have our being'—as we do in listening to or participating in today's tribal pop musics. The difference lies in the richness that accrues from Grainger's linear-harmonic polyphony. Three or four related tunes are usually singing simultaneously, and imperceptibly the tune itself changes through present *process*, increasing in grandeur and even in length. Recurrently, an incremental series of statements of the motif blows up in ecstatic whirligigs, so that we feel—as more gently and dreamily we do in *My Robin*—that we are moving in and out of time. The episodes always come back to the tune straight, with percussively chordal accompaniment; but each 'blowing up' is wilder than the previous one, until the tune itself grows frenzied, getting faster and faster, more corybantic. The end is an intensification of the stretto coda to *Shepherd's Hey*, though a real passacaglia is too august to collapse in an 'all fall down'. Indeed, stretto codas did not normally typify aristocratic passacaglias, which simply *went on*, like civilization, until—hopefully after a long time—they stopped. If there were a change of pulse at the end it would tend to be not faster, but slightly slower, proportionate to more spacious harmonies and a more architectonic disposition of the clauses. Civilized man likes to believe, or at least to pretend, that he is in control.

But this passacaglia of Percy Grainger—who had described his early music as a protest *against* civilization—has no doubt that it must get faster and faster, and does so in scintillating scoring that contributes to the orgiastic effect. The ultimate climax is unambiguous physical action, yet also a consummation attained in a large-scale concert piece. Like a few other examples we've referred to, it 'brings the house down' because it is not of its nature music to be passively listened to, but to be participated in. This is even more evident in the version for two pianos, six hands, made in 1919. In this country dance, unfolding in unbroken energy for well over six hundred bars, the polyphonic interlacing of the theme and its counter-themes is always luminous, while the 'explosions' sound the more exuberant because they are so directly a product of the players' physical activity at the keyboards. The up-tempo coda dizzies the mind and prickles the scalp. Grainger's demotic democracy is palpable in the delight generated by so many things, different yet the same, fitting together with such easy amicability. That easiness deserves to be called genius.

Grainger himself thought, and was right to think, that his ultimate masterpiece was not *Green Bushes* but the suite for wind-band which he charmingly called *A Lincolnshire Posy*. Five of the six folk-songs gathered together for the suite had been collected on the famous field-trip in 1905/6, and some of them he had used before, in sundry guises. The metaphor is appropriate in that it involves a reference to the (dis)guising indulged in by morris dancers who, touring the community, might present themselves in mythic identities, often with origins in an ancestral past. This particular, definitive, work was, however, composed in 1937, in the wake of Grainger's experience of American wind-bands, and must have been, at once unconsciously and consciously, a fusion of Percy's present with his past. For he regarded each movement as a 'portrait' of the singer who had first sung it to him, back in rural Lincolnshire in 1905. Inevitably, the singer was a part of Grainger's own and of England's past: which could be validly re-created, com-posed or put together, thirty years later, in an American New World. None of Grainger's works can more literally be described as re-creation; in none are 'instinct' and 'art' more closely identified.

In his fascinating preface to the published score Grainger speaks movingly of his memories of the 'old kings and queens of song' who had sung the tunes to him.

No concert singer I have ever heard approached these rural warblers in variety of tone-quality, range of dynamics, rhythmic resourcefulness and individuality of style. For while our concert singers (dull dogs that they are with their monotonous mooing and bellowing between *mf* and *ff* and with never a *pp* to their name) can show nothing better (and often nothing as good) as slavish obedience to the tyrannical behests of composers, our folksingers were lords of their own domain—were at once performers and creators. For they bent all songs to suit their personal artistic tastes and personal vocal resources; singers with wide vocal range spreading their intervals over two octaves, singers with small vocal range telescoping their tunes by transposing awkward notes an octave down . . . But even more important than these art-skills and personality-impresses is the heritage of old high moods of our race (tangible proofs that 'Merrie Englande'—that is agricultural England—once existed) that our yeoman singers have preserved for the scrutiny of mournful, mechanized, modern man.

At that point Percy indulges in one of his jeremiads about the evils of industrialism; but recovers his composure to introduce the singers from whom, so many years ago, he had garnered the tunes.

The first number combines two closely related songs, 'Dublin Bay' and 'Lisbon', sung by a Mr Deane in Brigg Workhouse. The matron thought the old man's heart too tremulous to sustain the nervous and physical strain of singing, but Percy eventually prevailed, and the tune proves to be far from ailing, but brisk, with military associations with the Duke of Marlborough. The mode of the main tune is Mixolydian A flat, but the counterpointed tune in an inner part is Lydian, creating a bimodality (rather than bitonality) tingling with false relations (see Example 23). The rhythm is a galloping 6/8, and the wryness of the harmony enhances, rather than weakens, the music's energy. But the independent strands of melody grow more polytonally ambiguous until the main tune is reaffirmed in canonic treatment, bolstered by repeated-note ostinatos. The delayed final cadence—tenths chromatically undulating before resolving in an upward, not downward, suspension—opens vistas, encapsulating in its relation to sixteenth-century procedures the piece's teetering between past and present (see Example 24).

Example 23 *Lincolnshire Posy*, 1. 'Lisbon Bay', opening, two–piano version.

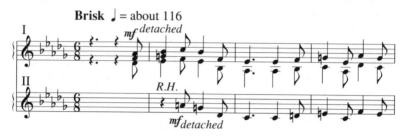

'Horkstow Grange' was sung by George Gouldthorpe, whose face and trunk were 'gaunt and sharp-cornered like a Norwegian peasant', but whose voice could haver between the harsh and the 'caressingly tender'. Then aged 66, and worn down by drudgery, he was 'kingly' in bearing, and his tune is invested with nobility. Grainger notes it in the Aeolian mode on A flat, in a slowly

Example 24 *Lincolnshire Posy*, 1. 'Lisbon Bay', ending

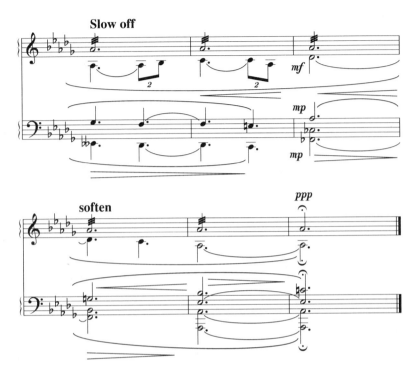

flowing common-time that, in George's singing and in Percy's
transcription of it, occasionally adds or omits a beat. The harmony is at first in austere diatonic concords, but in the varied
repeats for the subsequent stanzas it grows grander and more
awe-ful, with bitonality between triads of A flat and F flat. In the
two-piano version fearsome and fearful 'woggles' abound, persist-
ing into the unresolved cadence (see Example 25).

'Rufford Park Poachers' was sung by the great Joseph Taylor,
of 'Brigg Fair' fame. Grainger's favourite singer, he was unique
among them in being literate, as well as having an omnivorous
memory for tunes, if not for words. He had sung in his village-
church choir for more than forty years, which was unusual for an
agrarian folk-singer. Although 75 when he sang to Percy, he
betrayed no dimming of vocal powers, being 'a past master of
graceful, bird-like ornament'. Sturdy and robust, he was 'the soul
of gentleness, courtesy and geniality'. Grainger rewards him with
the longest movement and most wonderful music, the tune being
in the Phrygian mode on C, but with seconds and sixths often

Example 25 *Lincolnshire Posy*, 2. 'Horkstown Grange', ending, two-piano version.

sharpened. Probably it is not in 'a' mode but in the all-purpose folk-mode that Grainger often referred to (see p. 74). Grainger's original notation of the melody in 1905 may be revealingly juxtaposed with his re-creation of it (Example 26*a* and *b*), when the tune is heard in wide-spaced canon, delicately ornamented in accord with Taylor's example. Repeated, it is accompanied by a darkly scored, hesitant, halting figure. Out of syncopation, agitation is born; while some version of the tune, often modally altered, is always audible in octave doublings, interior chromatics grow wilder and stranger, on the verge of tonality. Canons again steer the polyphony towards stability, and the harmony settles on a drone chord of D flat, while the tune adheres to its nodal point of C. In the final bars, however, it declines to B flat: which may be thought of in modern terms as relative minor to the D flat drone chord, or in archaic folk terms as an oscillation between

**Example 26**  'Rufford Park Poachers' *a* as sung by Joseph Taylor and
notated by Grainger;
*b* opening of Grainger's two-
piano version, third movement
of *Lincolnshire Posy*.

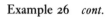

**Example 26** *cont.*

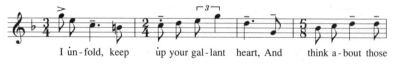

I un-fold, keep up your gal-lant heart, And think a-bout those

poa - chè - rs bold, that night in Rö - fut Park.

**Flowingly** ♩ = about 132

modal nodal points a tone apart. Significantly, this lonesomely heroic piece sounds, in its melismatically ornamented, near-heterophonic lines, at once the most archaic number in the suite and the most 'modern' in effect.

'The Brisk Young Sailor' was sung by a Mrs Thomson from Liverpool, but then living in Barton-on-Humber. Grainger tells us nothing else about her; perhaps she was a simple type, like her song, which is briskly youthful to match the sailor, returning to wed his true love. The key is straight B flat major, with a bouncy tune in triple time. Here Grainger's art lies in the electricity generated by the relation between metre and rhythm, which stimulates in being unpredictable. Bandsmen need considerable virtuosity to negotiate these skirling arabesques, though it appears that even with brisk young sailors things aren't as simple as they seem. The coda, fierce in its falsely related concords, wails chromatically to its final cadence, which remains unresolved (see Example 27).

'Lord Melbourne' was sung by George Wray, described by Percy as 'a relatively worldly and prosperous-coloured personality'. Although 80 years old when he sang for Grainger, he still gave evidence that he had been a much esteemed dancer, always to the fiddle. He held that folk-singing had been ruined by the habit of singing in church and chapel choirs, which required conformity to written notation and to an ensemble; on top of that the ubiquity of the equal-tempered piano destroyed the instinctive sense of pitch. Belligerent in his (unequal!) temperament, he appropriately sings a war-song, investing it with 'swift touches of swagger' and 'queer hollow vowel sounds (doubtless due to his lack of teeth)'. The boisterous folk-humour enhances, rather than mollifies, the song's grimness, and Grainger emulates the spasmodic irregularity of Wray's singing by notating the piece with no, or with constantly shifting, bar-lines. The song disturbingly fluctuates between 'free' and 'strict' sections, the former in massive homophony with strongly percussive dissonances, the latter in the Dorian mode, with volatile time-signatures and varied textures. The quixotic effect of the music no doubt amounts to a vivid impression of the man. Again there's a balance between tradition and the individual talent: the past (tradition) induces awe, for it goes on; but the present too is awe-ful since it is—if a man like George Wray be around—unpredictable, revealing strangeness beneath what might have been habit (see Example 28). While

Example 27  *Lincolnshire Posy*, 4. 'The Brisk Young Sailor', ending, two-piano version.

purely musical considerations govern the structure of these consummately written pieces, they thus preserve, as does all Grainger's music, a direct relationship to 'life'. In this case not only the character of the singer but also the unheard words affect the wayward expressivity of lines and harmonies. The two-piano version woggles to dramatic effect.

The last number, 'The Lost Lady Found', is the only one not originally notated by Grainger. It is a real dance-song or 'ballet', and Grainger's version has been discussed in its earlier form for solo voice and piano and/or other instruments (see p. 82). Grainger probably revived it as finale to his suite because it makes so triumphal a consummation; the new version is an independent piece, superbly devised for the medium. The tune is first presented in vigorous unison in an unadulterated Dorian mode, punctuated by percussively explosive, but consonant, chords.

Example 28  *Lincolnshire Posy*, 5. 'Lord Melbourne', bars 49–53, two-piano version.

Again, the music grows more mysterious as it becomes more polyphonically complex. The tune hides within undulating harmonies; flows into linear chromatics; and as climax is metrically disrupted. There is no grand peroration; the music, in true folk spirit, having proceeded in an unbroken pulse, simply stops, the lady having been found. That a quest is ended makes a fine conclusion to the cycle: in which the sequence of six movements is cunning, growing in intensity towards the apex of Joseph Taylor's elemental song, then unwinding back to relative normality. After the unexpected Happy Ending, life goes on, as best it may.

All the pieces so far discussed in this chapter are remarkable for their individual identity—no-one but Grainger could have made them—yet they are also inconceivable without the folk material they sprang from. *A Tribute to Foster*—written in 1913–16 and scored in 1931 for soloists, chorus, orchestra, and musical glasses and bowls—is People's Music in a rather different sense. It is private in being based on tunes by Stephen Foster that Rose used to croon to Percy when he was a child; but public in the sense that Foster was an American newspaperman who, working in the mid-nineteenth century in drearily industrial Pittsburgh, discovered a knack of writing songs that went straight to the heart of the man-in-the-street. Most of these songs were based on stock types of light music familiar in Pittsburgh parlours, owing much to British ballads of the type current in the eighteenth century's Vauxhall Gardens, and something to French *opéra comique*, vaudeville, and valse, to Viennese waltz, and to early romantic Italian opera. Foster's obliviousness of academic technique gave the mixture a guileless charm, notwithstanding the songs' obsession with dead or dying mothers and maidens, and with doggedly faithful Fidos. Once in a while cliché is irradiated, so that numbers such as 'Gentle Annie', 'Sweetly she sleeps' or 'Ah, may the red rose live alway' may send a furtive tear trickling down even the world-weariest cheek. Since it is difficult to explain how this alchemy occurs, one falls back, as did Percy, on the word 'genius'.

In one case, however, one may trace a relationship between effect and cause. Foster's loveliest song is surely 'Jeannie with the light brown hair', in which his words preserve poetic fragrance, along with distant memories of eighteenth-century diction. Both the freshness and the elegance of the words communicate themselves to the music, for the tune haunts with the simplicity of a Scots or Irish folk-song, its melodic pentatonicism being uneffaced by the rudimentary harmony (tonic, subdominant, dominant, tonic), or by the fragile artifice of the form, with a cunning minicadenza to waft us back to the da capo. We cannot doubt that the emotive effect of this song depends partly on the fact that Jeannie—unlike all those routinely anonymous Annies—was a real woman; in spite of being 'like a vapour', she was Stephen's wife, whom he could see as lovely and merry only through a 'soft summer haze' because their marriage was a failure. He lost his Jeannie—the mother to whom he was congenitally tied probably saw to it that he did—and succumbed to ill health and alcoholism, dying in a New York slum. His life is a cautionary tale, for commercial success was bound to obliterate the amateur minstrel. Others reaped material profit from Foster's world-wide fame.

That fame, however, was due not so much to his sentimental

ballads as to his fortuitous invention of what he called his 'Ethiopian songs'; later changing the term, no more accurately, to 'Plantation numbers'. These were based not on real Negro music but on the numbers of the Christy Minstrel shows, which were an exploitation of the Negro by white men with blackened faces, in an idiom closer to white ballad, march, and hymn than to black Gospel music, let alone the blues. The stylization of the Christy Minstrel show crystallized the white myth of the white-toothed, red-lipped, wide-grinning nigger, lazy and 'good for nothing', albeit 'without a care in the world'. The minstrel show took the savagery out of the black man's jollity, making him a figure of fun: while at the same time it related his homesickness, his sense of oppression, to the frustration inherent in every man, whatever the colour of his skin—especially in a raw industrial society that knew but obscurely where it was going. The minstrel show became a theatrical representation of the American Dream: which accounts for its prodigious appeal. Foster's Ethiopian songs distilled the dream's essence, being based on yearning for the Good Old Days, which were good because they were true, and were true because they were innocent. But they were not innocent as real folk music is innocent, since they expressed modern man's *consciousness* of loss. This is why the technique of such songs as 'The Old Folks at Home' and 'My Old Kentucky Home' is at once childish and artificial; and is also why these songs swept over the entire industrialized world. 'The Old Folks at Home' was translated into twenty-eight languages, including Japanese(!), and has been performed on all conceivable and a few nearly inconceivable combinations of voices and instruments. Presumably it owes its appeal to its rudimentariness: the fourfold-repeated clauses make their effect because they are *worth* repeating, or seem to be, as they cradle us into cosy regression. Bridges, parks, stadia, roses, lilies were named after Stephen Foster; medallions were struck in his honour.

Now Grainger himself, although a musician of considerable technical ability, was also, like 'primitive' Foster, fired by hedonism and nostalgia. Small wonder that he should have found inspiration in the work of this American Common Man, who peddled the dreams of the inarticulate in the mass civilization of industrial cities as well as, or more than, in small-town and rural America. Here was a link between Grainger's re-creation of The Old World's past and the Global Village he lived in. That both Foster and Grainger had obsessive, possibly pathological, relationships with their mothers adds to the piquancy. Percy's specially invented words, smuggled into his *Tribute to Foster*, explicitly tell us that 'When I was a tot on my mammy's knee | She sang dat race-track song to me,| Sung it to me sweet as a lullaby, | Hear dat song till de day I die.' In suburban Australia Rose had crooned Foster's song as she dandled her blue-eyed boy; grown up, and an American citizen, Grainger fashions from his memories this *Tribute to Foster*, assimilating the newly emergent pop music of America's New World to the folk traditions of the Old World that had been his mainspring to creation. This little scene is a present moment that is also memory and dream: as is most movingly evident in the 'Lullaby' that is the work's tender heart.

The 'Lullaby' is based on Foster's 'Camptown Races', one of the jauntiest of the Ethiopian songs, evoking that eupeptic if blackened face. In Grainger's version, however, the song sounds the saddest, most pathetically vulnerable thing in the world: not so much because a perky tune is played slowly, but because a discreet inner passing note or a delicate extension or contraction of a rhythm magically changes the perspective. The effect is the more mysterious because the exquisitely spaced chromatic part-writing is haloed with the ethereal tinkling of musical glasses tuned to Grainger's favourite F sharp major triad. In the piano-solo version the musical glasses are atmospherically emulated by Percy's 'woggling' tremolandos, and the key is, of course, F sharp major, carrying its customary hints of wonder and transcendence (see Example 29). As we have noted, such experience is not for Grainger, as it was for Bruckner or Messiaen, 'mystical' in an overtly religious sense, but is rather evocative of memory and dream, especially in relation to his mother. Still, mother-love is a basic experience, and the deeply moving effect of this little piece may bear on the reasons why Foster's apparently trite and cheerful tune has been so meaningful to thousands or millions of people in an industrialized world. If Grainger can reveal such pathos in it, perhaps it was never quite what it seemed; its jollity always contained wellsprings of sorrow not merely for until-recently enslaved black folk, but for all variously isolated and alienated people in big cities, unsure of direction, or even of identity. Grainger's genius audibly demonstrates how the blackened white face is a mask; and perhaps the piano version moves us most because it is literally a tear-jerker that cannot be accused of sentimentality since the

Example 29 'Lullaby' from *Tribute to Foster*, p.18.

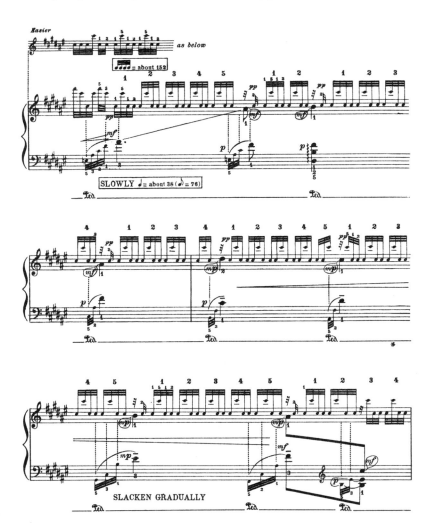

emotion is not in excess of the object. Indeed, the effect of the small piece complements that of the tenor-and-chorus setting of 'Brigg Fair'. In both, personal and universal feeling coexist: the universality of 'Brigg Fair' was that of the pre-industrial Folk; more surprisingly but no less affectingly, the 'Lullaby' discovers a complementary universality in our post-industrial world.

In this context the scoring of the full version of *Tribute to Foster* is of some significance. The soloists and chorus make it a communal activity, a get-together of like-minded people; the orchestra may bring in professional music-makers in a concert situation, though Grainger is careful to tell us that for home use a piano or harmonium may be substituted for orchestra; finally, the musical glasses and bowls offer scope for *ad hoc* amateurism, and might be played by kids and even tinier tots. To 'realize' the full poetic and musical effect of the glasses—sounded by fingers touching their moistened rims—calls for some skill: which young people are capable of, if imaginatively encouraged. Strokes of a double-bass bow drawn across a metal marimba, vibraphone, or vibraharp are effects now familiar in 'schools music', though they were far from familiar when Percy used them in this and other works written during the First World War. They enhance the magic, until the music fades out of time and space as a second group of glass-players is instructed, in Ivesian style, distantly to improvise 'any discordant or out of tune pitches'. Contralto solo, singing Percy's additional words, tells us that this song is 'Gwine still be sung's long as de worl's heart's young'. Perhaps that won't be very long, since Percy Pucks don't flourish in our increasingly competitive and materialistic societies. Even so, the lullaby defines an essential Grainger theme. In it, Grainger's democratic modernity functions not only between past and present, but also between age-groups, class-groups, and race-groups (the lullaby is in black and white), in an increasingly pluralistic, polymorphous community.

*Tribute to Foster* thus provides a link to our next chapter, which is about Grainger's remakings of past art- rather than folk-musics, in the interests of the always-volatile present.

# 7

# PRESENTING THE PAST

## *The Transcriptions and Concert-Paraphrases*

We have suggested that Grainger's importance may lie not so much in his being a composer as in his being a music-activator in a changing world. In the early and middle twentieth century he was aware, at once intuitively and by intellectual acumen, of what were to become crucial issues in the evolution of music in society. Nowadays, given the plethora of recordings of music of all ages and most places, we have no excuse for confining our attention to a niggardly two hundred years of European music. None the less it is remarkable that quite early in the century, and prolifically during the thirties and forties, Grainger had produced performing editions of a wide variety of European music from the Middle Ages to the seventeenth century. His versions did not, of course, seek what we would call authenticity; more basically, they aimed to make the music audible in terms we were familiar with, using modern instruments with an immediacy that overrides barriers between past and present. Grainger's arrangements of Early Music thus follow principles typical of his own composition; and—again, as with his own composition—their 'elastic scoring' encourages the use of such instruments as may come to hand. What matters is that one enjoys the act of singing, blowing, or bowing.

A series of anonymous medieval pieces—'Alleluia psallat', 'Angelus ad virginem', 'Beata viscera', 'Fulget coleistis curia', and 'Foweles in the frith'—are presented for solo or choric voices mixed or unmixed, with or without choirs of strings, woodwind, saxophones, and recorders, and with or without 'tuneful percussion'. At the time the educational value of these arrangements must have been considerable in schools and colleges of the United States, where some of them were published. Grainger also issued a repertory of ecclesiastical and secular music of the Renaissance: for instance, some now-famous but then-unknown works such as Dunstable's 'O Rosa bella', 'Regina Coeli' and 'Veni Sancte Spiritus', as well as pieces by an impressive array of composers including Machaut, Leonel Power, Dufay, Le Jeune, Willaert, Cabezon, and Dowland. The vernality of the delectable sonorities, mingling voices, saxophones, brass, wind and string choirs, tuned percussion, pianos, and harmonium may have little to do with scholarship; but the restored music lives, especially for young people, and it is not surprising that at least two of Grainger's dishings up—an anonymous 'Marionette douce' and Claude le Jeune's 'La Bel Aronde'—became popular, if not exactly best-sellers. Maybe we don't need them any more; but possibly we do, for they bring within the range of amateur performance old music that in the moment becomes new. There are parallels with Orff's *Schulwerk*, though Grainger offers richer musical rewards.

No less valuable was Grainger's resuscitation of English string music of the seventeenth century, now recognized as one of England's glories but then unknown outside the relatively cloistered groves of the Dolmetsch Festival, where performances, if presumptively authentic, were not always technically adequate. Grainger produced working editions of fantasias and dance-suites by composers such as Alfonso Ferrabosco, William Lawes, John Jenkins, and Henry Purcell himself long before most of them were known to the BBC, let alone to the generality of performing musicians. Nor were his scorings restricted to (modern) strings, for he suggested, indeed encouraged, substitutions of woodwind, brass, and saxophone choirs, and even pianos, for the original viols. A version of a Purcell fantasia for 'massed pianos' sounds bizarre but perhaps ought to be sampled, for many of Grainger's startling scorings have proved remarkably effective in active use. Grainger's success must be attributable to his native musicality and acute ear. He was not primarily concerned with historicity, since he believed, with the great Henry Thoreau, that

the *living* fact commemorates itself. Why look in the dark for light? . . . But one veil hangs over past, present and future, and it is the province of the historian to find out not what was, but what is. Where a battle has been fought, you will find nothing but the bones of men and beasts; where a battle is being fought, there are hearts beating.

When we sing and/or play a Grainger-arranged piece of Early Music we are in the mêlée of battle, as we are when we perform his magic re-enactments, such as *Scottish Strathspey, Shallow Brown, My Robin is to the Greenwood gone, A Lincolnshire Posy* or *A Tribute to Foster*. In this sense, the past *can* be presented.

We may better understand the relationship between Grainger's performance and his com-position if we listen to the arrangement he made, for solo piano, of the medieval Annunciation carol, 'Angelus ad Virginem', this being part of the collection of *English Gothic Music* he prepared in association with Dom Anselm Hughes. On the face of it, a modern grand piano would seem an improbable substitute for a small concourse of medieval voices; yet what is remarkable about this piece is that it continues to sound like medieval vocal music while also being effective as piano music. The tune is presented—again the verb is operative— three times: first in octave unisons; then in bell-like treble regis- ter, with a minimum of contrary motion in the purely diatonic parts; and finally in a low-registered organum of parallel octaves, fourths, and fifths, all godly intervals. Anyone who had heard no medieval music would know from this piano piece what at least this aspect of it is *in essentia*. Making a delightful recital piece, it is also literally a revelation.

More audacious than this medieval reconstitution is the lovely meditation on Dowland's ayre, 'Now, O now, I needs must part', made for piano in 1937. The melody is presented in close harmony, with tender dissonant suspensions, as in the piano ver- sion of 'Sussex Mummers' Christmas Carol'. At first the har- mony is identical with Dowland's, and the piano figuration, especially in the cadences, echoes lute conventions, though the second clause of the ayre is more fully scored. When the tune is repeated, however, as though for the second stanza, the figuration flows pianistically, or even quasi-orchestrally, and the chromatic harmony, if Delian, is quintessential Grainger. A quo- tation from the close (Example 30) will indicate the depth, but also the 'linearity', of Grainger's harmonization. Here the music has acquired a dual identity, being at once Dowland reborn, and Grainger identified with him. For the moment, Grainger is Dowland's 'guise', and the old England (which Percy loved) and the new England (which he thought he despised) have no need to be at odds. Something not far from this happens, more dis- creetly, in the piano version of Byrd's variation-set on the pop (not folk) tune, 'The Carman's Whistle'. Grainger's 'discretion' lies in the fact that he leaves Byrd's sequence of variations, much of his ornamentation, and most of his harmony unmodified. Even so, the piece seems to be refashioned through its cunning disposition on the keyboard, and comes out as an

Example 30 'Now, O now, I needs must part', ending.

'original' jointly produced by two composers chronologically separated by three hundred years.

As one might expect, the most important category among
Grainger's transcriptions of other people's music is his dishings-
up of Bach, who had so powerfully conditioned Percy's approach
to part-writing and to 'long flow form'. Some of his Bach
arrangements serve the same function as do his versions of
medieval and Renaissance music; if people, especially young people, play a Prelude and Fugue from the Forty-eight, or a movement from a Brandenburg Concerto, or an organ chorale prelude
on (say) 'four pianos as an octave study', or on choirs of woodwind, brass, or strings, or on 'string four-some' or 'saxophone six-
some', the music will come to them as though new-minted;
understanding may be opened, or reopened, along with the ears.

Larger-scaled works were produced by transcribing organ works for the piano, on the model of Busoni, one of Grainger's heroes. Especially remarkable is the dishing-up of the famous Toccata and Fugue in D minor, wherein Percy absorbs the juiciest bits of both Busoni's and Tausig's versions into his own exuberant recreation. This makes for a confusing manuscript and an extremely difficult piece; but Martin Jones's recorded performance surely emulates Grainger's performances in persuading us that the sense of *danger* is inherent in the music. For we must remember that Bach's toccatas were 'touch' pieces that transferred to the relatively mechanical organ the humanly theatrical panache of operatic recitative and arioso, the physical energy of body movement, the glamorous colours of baroque organ registration, and the impetuosity of flying fingers and frisking feet. Bach's organ toccatas, especially those of his youth, were of their nature exhibitionistic, designed to 'show off' modern man's passionate powers in secular as well as ecclesiastical contexts. They were also show-music in a technical sense, intended to 'try out the lungs' of an instrument consisting of an array of wind-blown pipes. Bach, an expert on organ construction, was often asked to advise churches on the disposition of a new instrument. Demonstrating its qualities, he is said to have improvised with hair-raising and ear-boggling abandon. Grainger's transcription of the D minor Toccata and Fugue makes just such an effect; because, not in spite of, its outrageousness, the Grainger version has an authenticity which, if not historical, is live on the mark. Again, 'the living fact commemorates itself'.

An even more 'outrageous' example is Grainger's version of the famous-notorious *Toccata in F*, which Percy dishes up from organ for three pianos, six hands, or alternatively for 'massed pianos'(!) Given the corybantic character of this extraordinary piece, one imagines that the sheer visceral assault of the massed pianos might be to the musical point; though often—in, for instance, the transcription of the A minor fugue for eight hands on two pianos or for 'massed pianos'—the purpose of multiplication seems to be to achieve greater clarity rather than to make the music louder. Occasionally Grainger crosses the boundary between arrangement and composition in dealing with Bach, as with folk music. 'Blithe Bells' he describes as a 'free ramble' around 'Sheep may safely graze', presenting it in 1932 in elastic scoring for room-music fifteen-some, or wind-band, or an orchestra as full as might be available. He also made versions for piano solo and for four hands on two pianos. Even the solo-piano version (see Example 31) is so radiantly disposed on the keyboard that the interweaving of the *cantus firmus* through the surrounding parts is always clear, while leaving room for resonating campanology. The two-piano version is even more opulent, though always and appropriately as clear as a bell. In all the versions Grainger does not confine himself to Bach's harmony, but uses it as a launching-pad for his own, often highly chromatic, idiom. If the harmony is not Bach's the rich lucidity of the part-writing is profoundly Bachian, and should cause no offence to men of good will: who will accept Grainger's invitation to ramble with Bach's bell-tinkling sheep along our own winding mossy ways, in early twentieth-century Britain.

Example 31    'Blithe Bells', piano version, part of p. 6.

In pieces like 'Blithe Bells' and 'Now, O now' Grainger effects his miracle of dual identity. In a different class as well as category are a number of arrangements of the type that nineteenth-century composer-pianists used to call 'concert paraphrases'. Percy's most direct contribution to the genre is his *Paraphrase on Tchaikovsky's Flower Waltz from the Nutcracker Suite*, made in 1905, to take on tour: a barnstorming piece more hilarious than breath-taking, though one suspects that Percy chuckled at it himself. The

*Ramble on Love*, a meander around the love-duet from Act III of Strauss's *Rosenkavalier*, is more artful in more than one sense. Meticulously notated and exquisitely written, it sounds like streamlined Liszt, refashioned in Ravellian lucidity, and is a marvellous instance of Grainger's irresistible way with a piano. But although Grainger claimed to relish Strauss's opera, and to approve of the 'vulgarity' of his music in general, it was perhaps too close to the Teutonic mainstream for Percy to attain the true 'mind-mating' that he found in his versions of Dowland's ayre and Bach's chorale prelude. He comes nearer in the two-piano fantasy on Gershwin's *Porgy and Bess*, which gets the best of several worlds in being luxuriously laid-out concert music of which the material is at once black American folk music and white American show-music. As we might expect, Grainger's admiration for Gershwin was heartfelt. He made a number of concert arrangements of individual Gershwin tunes, including a ravishing one of the classic Gershwin number, 'The Man I love'. The idiom is close to that of Gershwin's own piano arrangements, more craftily turned.

But the most convincing of Grainger's 'concert paraphrases' is his version of Stanford's *Four Irish Dances*, which had originally been orchestral works of their composer, an Irishman who loved Brahms. Being in origin folk music, these dances were grist to Grainger's mill, out of which he makes brilliant works for concert use, ebulliently folky in spirit if without the 'folk presence'—the ritual enactment—typical of his rambles and meanders. Stanford, despite his Teutonic, Brahmsian bias, had a genuine interest in and fondness for Irish folk-song, and Grainger admitted a debt to his researches. Here, paying homage to Stanford, he makes effective art music in its own right: more convincingly than he does when making piano versions of orchestral works of Delius. These were undertaken, of course, because he held the music in peculiar affection, and wanted to assist in its dissemination at a time when orchestral performances, not to mention recordings, were infrequent. Delius was thrilled with Grainger's two-piano version of *A Song of the High Hills*, made in 1933, and was scarcely less enthusiastic about the transcriptions of smaller works like the *First Dance Rhapsody*. The arrangements are indeed skilful, but at this date can be dispensed with: as can, more readily, the potted versions of Famous Piano Concertos (the Grieg, the Schumann, Tchaikovsky no. 1, and Rachmaninov no. 2) that Percy made to play on his recital tours. Although it is unlikely that he picked up any hints from Alkan's astonishing Concerto for piano solo, these rehashes create, with dizzying ingenuity, a similar illusion of soloist and tutti simultaneously rampant. Despite this technical interest, there is no longer any justification for these concoctions; and there can never have been *much* justification, for Percy himself called them 'bleeding chunks', and seems to have used them as what we would call 'trailers', encouraging people to attend the big orchestral event, next week or whenever. They could have had no function as popularizing Best Bits of this or the other work, being far too difficult for amateurs to tackle at home.

A long way from these trailers are a few transcriptions of well-known songs by Fauré, a composer whose civilized refinement seems some way from Grainger. Technically, however, Grainger battened on Fauré's subtle equilibrium between vocal line and piano-part; interweaving the voice-part over, through and under the dialoguing piano, much as he does in his piano versions of folk-songs, Percy creates from the sweet sensuality of 'Nell' and the elegiac gravity of 'Après un rêve' not 'concert paraphrases', but piano music of the loveliest lucidity. Even Grainger's slightest dishings up for piano are at least good fun to play. One thinks of his arrangements of music by his friends—not only the great Delius but also Balfour Gardiner, Goossens, and Cyril Scott, not to mention a clutch of songs by his wife Ella, who couldn't and didn't lay claim to talent. These efforts, which don't bolster Percy's reputation as a composer, foster his social and domestic image, being music for everyday use, by 'whom it may concern'.

Grainger's arrangements fall broadly into two categories. One may be called utilitarian in that such arrangements re-present music then considered obsolete or for varying reasons impracticable. The other category might be called exhibitionistic in that the music is tarted, as well as dished, up for display in concerts. Grainger was himself an exhibitionistic performer: so this would seem an appropriate point to comment on his pianism, in so far as we know of it from press and personal reports, and from Grainger's own writings about pianos and piano playing.

All reports indicate that Grainger's fame was attributable equally, and simultaneously, to his creative energy as composer and to his charisma as performer. When he first played in London, while still a teenager, the *Daily Telegraph* remarked that 'such genuine humour and wit, such enthusiasm, such virility, and such masterly musicianship as Mr Grainger showed are met with only on the rarest occasions in a musician of any country'. A Frankfurt critic referred to him as 'a poet at the piano! Here was no English coolness or dryness'; while on his first American appearance in the Aeolian Hall he was compared with Paderewski and Kreisler, and was congratulated on the enterprise of his programme-making. He was praised alike for his meticulous clarity in unfolding Bach's polyphony; for his command of large-scale structure in the Brahms Handel Variations; and for his mastery of ornament and colour in the music of Ravel and Albéniz. In all 'there is an agreeable absence of pedantry, and the vivacity of youth in everything he plays, banishing all possibility of boredom no matter what piece he has in hand'. It is good to know that critics immediately appreciated his insight into Grieg's folk-dance pieces opus 66 and opus 72: of which Grieg himself had remarked that 'he plays my Norwegian peasant dances as none of my own countrymen can play them. He has the true folk-poetry in him, and yet it is quite a long way from Australia to Norway.'

Composers savoured Percy's pianism even more readily than did critics. Grieg maintained that Grainger 'realized my ideals of piano playing. If I had his technique, my conception of piano playing would have been exactly the same. Like a god, he is lifted high over all suffering, all struggle. But one feels they have been there, but have been overcome'. Similarly, Delius confessed, in a letter to Percy, that 'I have seldom had such pleasure from piano playing as I have from yours. I find it extremely musical, masterly, without the slightest affectation or pose. Your delicate nuancing is quite a revelation to me.' While these composers were not disinterested, since there were close affinities between Grainger's music and their own, their enthusiasm seems to have been shared by most truly creative musicians, including Busoni, who was temperamentally at an opposite pole. The Norwegian composer Sparre Olsen summed up general opinion when he identified the vitality of Grainger's playing with his validity as a human being. 'He had no technical difficulties, he was a supreme master.' Even so, he never *tried* to be a master, 'other phases of piano playing being more important to him. His sense of tonal beauty, his variation and explanation of the musical material was fantastic', because he had 'mastered the whole scale of human feeling—the soft, the tender, the lyrical, the intensive, the dramatic, the wild'. Percy was, in other words, a 'natural'; and if this would not rebound so much to his credit were he active as a pianist today, so much the worse for us. We could do with more executive musicians for whom an instrument is literally instrumental, a means towards exploration and discovery, while also being a source of sheer pleasure and delight.

Although Grainger established his reputation as a pianist when he was very young, his charisma did not wane. During his forties and fifties he abandoned his monster tours and seldom performed in public. His impact on audiences remained, however, undimmed. As late as December 1946 we find the Montreal Gazette informing its readers that 'as a pianist Mr Grainger is formidable . . . No pianist before the public today, and add the biggest publicised names to this list, can surpass him. In fact, very few can equal him. In style, musicianship and authority, and in his strict observance of the composer's directions he is a master'. Oddly enough, Percy sometimes, especially in later life, affected to despise the piano because of its limitation to a single equal-tempered chromatic scale, as against the theoretically infinite scope of his Free Music (to be discussed in the next chapter). It is however improbable that Percy took this solemnly; certainly no pianist-composer did more to explore the possibilities the instrument offered, or more consistently made piano versions of his own creations. Sometimes these versions are more effective than the originals, in that they profit from the identity between composer and performer.

Even during his student days Grainger took the piano seriously enough to write about the new potential he found in it. Many consequences followed, he pointed out, from the fact that a piano is basically a percussion instrument—'a beating of felt hammers upon tightened wires'. This means that, for all the instrument's association with the rich and complex history of European polyphony and homophony, it also contains the most fundamental of sound-sources: which Debussy rediscovered when he included in his 'pianistic vocabulary many of the beautiful kaleidoscopic effects a gifted child strumming on the piano would produce, but which our overtrained ears have rejected in the past. Thus his methods have implied a study of the problem of just how much dissonance can be artistically applied and yet keep his work within the bounds of the beautiful.' Predictably, Grainger instances Debussy's fascination with the Javanese gamelan, and with effects related to bell-harmonics. That a sophisticated mechanical instrument like the piano also possessed this natural acoustic dimension must have gratified Percy, who was himself a 'gifted child', experimentally enlivening tradition.

But if there was still much to be learned about the piano's natural properties, its 'artificial' aspects had still not been adequately explored. Bach must have delighted in keyboard instruments, if not specifically the piano, because they were naturally polyphonic instruments also capable of the utmost complexity of harmony. According to Grainger, the technique of polyphonic playing on piano was still in its infancy, only Busoni having profoundly investigated the possibilities. Critics the world over seemed to think that in this respect Grainger equalled or even surpassed Busoni; and we have noted several examples of the care Grainger took to delineate precise degrees of stress in each melodic strand of his own compositions. Percy quotes the opening of his own 'Irish Tune from County Derry' as an example of his technique of 'middle voicing'. This is similar in principle to, but still more fastidious than, the example from 'The Sussex Mummers' Christmas Carol' quoted on page 67. A pop song, such as Gershwin's classic 'The Man I Love', prompts Grainger to no-less loving precision.

Polyphonic freedom, sensitively realized on a keyboard, calls for the kind of rhythmic subtlety that Grainger relished from early youth. A piano, being a one-man band, lends itself readily to rhythmic experimentation, and critics, writing of Grainger as pianist, frequently connected the 'mystery' of his part-playing with his rhythmic sensibility. A writer in the *Adelaide Register*, reviewing a concert in August 1924, wrote that 'to his wonderful hands nothing seems impossible'; and that 'those privileged to hear his 'Zanzibar Boat Song' will not soon forget the haunting rhythm and the wonderful interweaving of themes. It was altogether a wonderful recital.' That final *cri de cœur* eloquently testifies to Grainger's charisma. It would have been good to hear him, 'live' indeed.

But one doesn't get very near to that experience by way of the Duo-Art piano rolls that Larrikin Records, in association with the Australian Broadcasting Corporation, reproduced on LPs in 1977. The notes inform us that a 'reproducing piano' should not be confused with 'the earlier and inferior pianola', but the claim that the mechanical instrument is 'capable of reproducing every subtlety of tempo and dynamic nuance' cannot be substantiated on the evidence of these first re-recordings. The tone of the 'Steck Boudoir Grand *c.*1918' featured on a representative mixed programme of Grainger, Grieg, Delius, and Stanford is clattery in the extreme, and tonal continuity is spasmodic. The virtuosic version of Stanford's *Irish Dances* gives one a notion of what Grainger must have been like in full flight, but nowhere do we get any idea of the sensibility and tenderness commentators detected in his playing. 'Irish Tune from County Derry' as presented on this disc comes near to affronting modern taste, for Percy's rubato verges on the grotesque, and he seems to 'bring out the tune' only by relinquishing synchronicity between the tones of a chord. The arrangement of Delius's Brigg Fair, in so far as it is audible, is a disaster, and surely cannot resemble the performances that so thrilled Delius. One must presume that mechanical deficiencies are more to blame than Grainger's admired pianism.

Some support for this view is offered by a later disc devoted to Grieg, and revamped in 1982. The engineer, Dennis Condon, explains how he has worked to improve quality in four ways: by using more efficient pneumatic devices; by combining pneumatics with today's electric technology; and by building a device having 'fingers' and 'feet' that can be set before any piano, so that the Duo-Art performances can be improved by playing them on new pianos. Certainly the main difference between the 1977 'mixed' disc and the all-Grieg disc of 1982 is that the piano sonority of the latter is that of a modern Steinway. Grainger's playing here affords pleasure and none of the embarrassment typical of the earlier recording. The familiar *Peer Gynt* suite has all the rural vernality one could ask for, and a sustained quasi-orchestra line. The scherzoid passages sparkle, while cohering with the lyrical-harmonic textures. An especially telling comparison is possible because both discs include Grieg's opus 66. In the later version evenness of sonority and continuity of rhythm reveal something of the 'true folksong poetry' that Grieg himself admired in Percy's playing.

But perhaps the only recorded evidence of Grainger's piano-playing that gives a reasonably adequate notion of its quality is the performance of the Chopin B minor Sonata issued by Columbia in 1925, said to be the first complete recording of a sonata produced in the electrical recording era. Percy makes a few cuts and allows himself a sprinkle of wrong notes, but plays with a furious intensity that proves as revelatory of Chopin's wild Polish heart as it is of Grainger's own heroic ferocity. Having heard this, one can have no doubt that Grainger was among the supreme pianists of any time, even without the charisma added, in live performances, by his extravagant good looks. And as far as his own music is concerned, we may today at least get a vicarious idea of Percy's legendary pianistic abilities from the five CDs covering the *Complete Piano Music of Percy Grainger*, undertaken by Martin Jones for Nimbus. If Grainger in his arrangements and presumably his performances sometimes seems to have been 'possessed' by dead composers, whether it be an old man quavering a folk-song, or John Dowland singing to his lute, or J. S. Bach trying out the lungs of an organ, one may say that Martin Jones is likewise possessed by Grainger. The doggerel verse tells us that 'The Abbé Liszt | Banged the piano with his fist; | That was the way | He used to play'; and although there is of course much more than that to Jones's often exquisitely sensitive playing of Grainger, he may also create a comparable sense of activity at white heat. The reverberant acoustic favoured by Nimbus for the recordings—and deplored by some critics—adds to the illusion of present action. DANGER is in the offing, along with zest, unpredictability, waywardness and, above all, generosity and love. Jones makes us perch perilously on the edge of our seats, as Percy surely did, while at the same time he reminds us that when Grainger played, one was unaware of the mechanics of the instrument, or of the technique necessary to bend it to one's will. As Grieg put it, 'it is a human being, a great soul, an aristocrat that is playing'; and if it seems surprising to call a Boy from the Bush an aristocrat, one suspects that Grieg meant that Grainger's pianism was of purest blood. Martin Jones, intermittently raffish in his Graingerish exuberance, preserves that purity unsullied. These are vintage recordings which, in the guise of Grainger, are destined to acquire classic status.

## 8

# A 'GIFTED CHILD' LOOKS BACK
# TO THE FUTURE
### Grainger as Innovator and Educator

We have observed that Grainger's music involved the simultaneity of past and present. Overriding time and place, he also embraced the future—the effect of his present moments on what might happen next. If we concentrate only on his conscious experimentation during the last years of his life, we may be tempted to say that what he accomplished was not much; for although he had a brilliant mind, at once intuitive and intelligent, he was not a systematic theorist. A doer and maker, he lived vivaciously in the present on the fundaments of the past; if he sometimes looked over the rainbow, he was too busy making and doing to carry through an analysis of his hunches. In this respect Grainger's limitations may be the ultimate evidence of his wisdom.

How this might be so is latent in a fascinating short work that Grainger sketched out in two versions in 1911 and 1914. He called it *The Lonely Desert Man sees the Tents of the Happy Tribes*, and toyed with it on and off during his American years, intermittently knocking off a fresh version in hotel rooms on his peregrinations. The closest he came to a definitive version was made in 1949, and recast in 1950 and 1954. This is scored for three voices singing in a Grainger-invented pseudo-Amerindian language, accompanied by alto saxophone, clarinet, bassoon, trumpet, strings, two marimbas, two guitars, and piano. This combo hints at the piece's *ad hoc* state, in a limbo between concert music, folk music, pop, and ritual activity. While the piece doesn't pretend to be important music, its ambiguous status is significant and its autobiographical implications are crucial. Clearly, Grainger was thinking of himself as an itinerant Red or aboriginal Indian, cut off, in an industrial society, from the Happy Tribes of the Days of Yore. For the Amerindians of the piece these Happy Tribes were, of course, their ancestral clans, long obliterated by Progress; for Percy, they were his Australian forebears, the British Folk who had inspired so much of his creation, and to a lesser degree the folk of his new American home. All had been defiled by the rampant industrialism that Percy abominated.

The effect of the piece, on both audience and performers, tends to be, with its invented 'primitive' language, comic; yet it is also pathetic, even forlorn. *The Lonely Desert Man* starts off with a grand, near-pentatonic ululation, high and strained in tenor register, over a drone chord on G, 'woggling' through various dissonant shifts before cadencing, by way of a first-inversion dominant seventh of D flat, back to G major (see Example 32). The Happy

Example 32 *The Lonely Desert Man sees the Tents of the Happy Tribes*, opening.

Example 32  *cont.*

Tribes—'as if from afar, behind platform if possible'—answer the ululation with a 'primitive' male-voiced incantation in speech-rhythmed repeated notes, in what might be the Mixolydian mode with flattened sixth. They too sing in a comical invented language—or inarticulate bassoon, clarinet, and alto sax may deputize for them. Sopranos answer them with the same rudimentary (and perhaps therefore happy) rune-like tune, with an accompaniment of levelly repeated chords on guitars and/or similar strummed instruments. This accompaniment prophetically merges the primitive beat of Amerindian drums and rattles into the simulated and mechanized forms it assumes in the pretend-savagery of twentieth-century tribal pop. Solo baritone fades out on the deceptive flat sixth, so that when the music 'slows off lots' on chords of E flat with 'added' notes, it is disorientated from the 'home' key of G (see Example 33). This is forlorn too, as well as funny, suggesting that Grainger's experimentalism as a New Worlder was an attempt to rediscover a ritual such as had once animated these aboriginal Americans. In a society dedicated to a work-ethic, man needed to relearn how to play, for, as Karl Bücher had pointed out as early as 1901—when Percy was embarking on his early innovatory works—'play is older than work, art is older than production for use'. *The Lonely Desert Man* is indubitably play, yet it also asks questions about what it means to be human. Although the desert man is a comic guy as well as a guise, he allegorizes the basic concerns of Grainger's life: which sought for a universal music beyond categorized artistic traditions and was itself creative of the values men and women could and should live by. His ambition was as grand as it was simple.

It was also this paradoxical man's ultimate paradox. Throughout his life, while making his present music and remaking the past, Grainger tinkered with hunches whereby he hoped to create a music if not of 'the hills themselves', at least of Nature herself in so far as it was founded on natural laws and principles. How literally absurd—*ab surdo*, or 'from a deaf person'—it is that the acoustical fact of the octave should be divided into twelve equal semitones; why not the eighteen that Busoni propounded, or forty-three according to the prescription of Californian Harry Partch; or any other division that pertained to the present moment, and was audible in the world around us, in the yells of birds and beasts, the buzzing of insects, the soughing of wind in telegraph wires? Grainger's ultimate attempt to 'free' music was to be concentrated into the last years of his American life at White Plains, New York. Prophetic hints of it had, however, been evident from early years: in for instance 'Sea-Song', sketched in 1907, worked on in 1922 and 1946, but never brought to fruition. The piece was to auralize the sea, our first mother and surrogate for the unconscious, using microtonal pitches and beatless

rhythms since arithmetrical divisions of tones and metres are anti-Nature. Parallel to the aborted 'Sea-Song' is the 'Bush-Music', for which Grainger made sketches as early as 1900, and again in 1922. Presumably the intention was to evoke the quasi-silent emptiness of the Australian Bush, with minimum intervention from the human nervous system. Only fifteen bars are extant, almost all having a different time-signature. The fragment adds nothing to the *Hill Songs*, though it predictably suggests that bush is more openly amorphous in texture than hills.

Another of Grainger's exploratory notions was inspired not directly by Nature but by a man-made contrivance, the railway train. What fascinated Grainger, who was partial to lengthy rail-journeys, was not the train itself, but the disturbances to natural process caused by riding it. The immediate source of the experiment was a journey undertaken in 1901, 'in a very jerky train going from Genoa to San Remo'. Percy made jottings at the time, and over the years played with the idea on rail-trips he took across vast continents like Australia and America. Gearing his musical imagination to those spatial immensities, he envisaged an orchestra of gargantuan proportions, graded in accord with the two double bassoons and six bassoons at the base. Maybe this elephantiasis indicates that Grainger admitted that the project, given the complexity of its irregular rhythms, was unrealizable, though the fragment of orchestral score completed in 1976 by Eldon Rathburn, and available in photostat from the Grainger Archives, is exciting, at least to look at. It might be exciting to listen to also, for the 'simplified sketch' for piano that Grainger made as late as 1957 produces, in a mere thirty-five seconds, an alarming sense of rhythmic dislocation. Cyril Scott was right to point out, in his perceptive pioneer essay on Grainger of 1916, that the composer's experimental enterprise was an overflow from

his entire musical personality, for he exists as something quite new in musical expressivity; he has invented new forms and transformed old ones; he is a great harmonic innovator, yet unlike Schoenberg he does not lead us into the excruciating. Furthermore, although at times he is a little too unafraid of the obvious, he is entirely consistent therein and one sees at once how little such a thing is the outcome of weakness. In addition to all these characteristics, he can equally show forth a poetry and pathos which speak in sublime dulcitude to the soul and a rollicking liveliness which awakens energy almost in the limbs of the decrepit. For although Grainger has an intellect of which many a bookworm might be envious, it dwells side by side with a child-likeness as charming as it is surprising.

Scott maintained that Grainger's experimental works, had he been able to finish them, would have been masterpieces. It seems more probable that their 'incompletability' is the essence of their enterprise: though one of his innovations, the 'Random Round', at least attained such consummation as randomness permits. This venture was inspired by Percy's experience, during his New Zealand trip of 1912, of the Polynesian improvising polyphonists we have previously referred to (p. 50). 'The polyphony displayed by these four to eight singers', he comments,

was prodigious, and as the whole thing was prestissimo (Polynesian languages lend themselves very readily to speed) it reminded me of nothing so much as a seething, squirming musical ant-hill, bursting into furious song for sheer joy and high spirits. No doubt the habit of harmony here displayed had been caught long ago from missionary hymns, yet the use made by these brilliant musicians of their foreign accomplishment was completely native in its application and was governed by the individualistic dictates of Unwritten Music. Their procedure followed habits rather than laws—it will be seen that a great range of personal choice was left to all the members of this Rarotongan choir, in each of whom a highly complex, delicate and critical sense for ensemble was imperative. Each of these natives had to be a kind of improvising communal composer, and to a far greater degree simultaneously creative and executive than is the case with peasant songsters in Great Britain or Scandinavia . . . Attractive as are the passionate warmth of vocal colour, the savage exhilarating rattle of the rhythms, and the often almost wistful sweetness of the melodic phrases heard in this Rarotongan music, most fascinating of all to a modern composer are the Bach-like gems of ever-changing, euphoniously discordant polyphonic harmony which throughout surprise, baffle and soothe the ear; patches of concord alternating with whole successions of discords—mainly seconds.

(The general import of Grainger's alignment of his improvising Polynesians with Bach was discussed in a previous chapter: see pp. 48–50).

Grainger adds that while this free polyphony makes to our ears a 'seductive complex harmonic appeal', it was not heard by the native performers as harmony in the 'Western' sense. The process is more accurately described as heterophony wherein everyone 'voices' a 'heterogenously' different version of the same tune, the harmonic consequences being fortuitous and the more exciting for being unpredictable. When in 1914 Grainger evolved, from the practice of the Rarotongans, his notion of the 'Random Round' he called on not only voices, but also 'guitars and mandolins, to which could be added (if available) mandola, piano, xylophone, celesta, glockenspiel, resonaphone or marimbaphone, strings and wind instruments'. The round functioned, as did the music of the singing Polynesians and of the Balinese and Javanese gamelan players not so far away from Polynesia, on principles that encouraged communal participation. The 'round' comprised a number of sections (A, B, C, etc.)

each of which was again divided into as many as 10 to 20 variants (A1, A2 etc.), some quiet, some noisy, some simple, some complex; each bar of each variant being composed in such a way that it forms some sort of harmonic whole when performed together with any bar of any or all of the other variants of the same section. The guitars formed the background for all the rest, and as soon as they got going with section A any or all of the other players could fall in, when and how they pleased, with any of the variants of section A, provided their beats corresponded with those of the guitars. Before section B was begun, a Javanese gong would be beaten, whereupon the same sort of canonical intermingling of the different variants of B would be undertaken that had just occurred with the A variants; and so on with C, D etc., to the end. It will be seen that a fairly large range of personal choice was allowed to everyone taking part, and that the effectiveness of the whole thing would depend on the natural sense for contrasts of form, colour and dynamics displayed by the various performers, and their judgement in entering or leaving the general ensemble at suitable moments.

Grainger described the piece as a 'join-in-when-you-like round for a few voices and tone-tools, tone-backgrounded by a gut-strung guitar tone-wrought around 1912–14 in Holland and England'. 'Tone tools' is blue-eyed English for instruments, 'tone-backgrounded' means accompanied, and 'tone-wrought' means composed. In 1943 Grainger made a kind of score with verbal instructions. This is available in photostat from the Grainger Archives, and is worth study not only because the experiment works, but also because it is prophetic of the Indeterminacy practised in the fifties by John Cage and his associates, and of the Process or Minimal musics evolved during the sixties and seventies by Steve Reich, Terry Riley, and others. Percy grouped his verbal instructions under four headings: 1) Choice of part-takers—

which means the groups and ranges of instruments that might co-operate; 2) Form of the Round—which expands the account of how the round operates outlined above; 3) Duties of of the Band-Boss—which means a conductor who doesn't, of course, direct the music in the conventional expressive and interpretive sense, but simply acts as a co-ordinator, making decisions as to when 4) 'Change-shocks in tone-colour and tone-size shall be introduced'. The 'score', which is printed after the instructions, consists of seven pages of harmonic 'foreplay' for guitars, which pervades the whole round, plus the melodic and rhythmic figures and motives to be repeated and variously combined. They all more or less fit, as do the mainly pentatonic figures in Balinese music: either because the melodic figures oscillate around a nodal point, like many 'primitive' musics; or because harmonies are either static, over a drone, or move sequentially in cyclic (non) progressions that always return to the same point. These notations were not, of course, meant to be definitive, but were suggestions as to ways in which music might again be ongoing activity involving a commu-nity, rather than an act of communication from one human being (the composer) to others (the audience). This amounted to a social philosophy, as was indeterminacy for John Cage. It was also an educational principle derived from primitive musics, yet demon-strably applicable to our in-some-ways degenerate selves. This is evident in Grainger's comments on a particular performance of the 'Round' in London, in the summer of 1914. That Europe was about to be engulfed in the first of the World Wars adds piquancy to the social criticism inherent in Percy's enterprise:

Fifteen people were engaged in this experiment, and the results obtained were very instructive to me personally. Several of those taking part quickly developed the power of merging themselves into the artisitic whole, and whereas at the outset the monotonous babel pro-duced somewhat resembled 'a day at the Dogs' Home, Battersea' (as a leading critic once described Albéniz's marvellous and touching piano piece *Jerez* when I first introduced it to London audiences), after a little practice together the whole thing took on form, colour and clarity, and sounded harmonious enough, though a frequent swash of passing disso-nances was noticeable also. I look forward to some day presenting to English and American audiences a performance of this blend of modern harmonic tendencies with experiences drawn from the improvised polyphony of primitive music, although, of course, my piece represents only the veriest beginning of what may ultimately be evolved in the realms of concerted improvisation.

So it proved: for Grainger's 'Random Round' was succeeded by other tintinnabulating round-games played by the 'tuneful percussion' of Carl Orff's *Schulwerk*, and then by the more-or-less genuine Balinese and Javanese gamelans whose seraphic sounds have become familiar through thousands of schools and colleges in the United States, and are now percolating into Britain and other outposts of industrial civilization. It is easy to say that the culture and philosophy implicit in these musics are so remote from those of our Western technocracies that interest in them can be no more than a form of escape. Yet Grainger had demonstrated, all those years ago, that there is a positive aspect to such non-competitive communal activity, in which anyone may democratically participate to the level of his or her ability. Doing so, one may discover that one's ability far exceeds one's expectation.

The forward-looking aspects of Grainger's 'Random Round' of 1914 were not merely educational. Not only have the young taken readily to such notions; there is now also a school of West Coast American composers, led by Lou Harrison, who construct their own oriental yet indigenous gamelans, and make for them modern American music that does indeed, like the ancient Balinese art, 'cherish, conserve, consider, create'. Such is not far from the philosophical and social ambitions that Grainger nursed for his own music, aspects of which anticipate not only the Minimalists who have flourished from the sixties, but before them the Canadian composer Colin McPhee, who went to live in Bali, and made transcriptions of gamelan music. He also wrote the definitive scholarly work on the philosophy and techniques of Balinese music, adapting some of its principles to Western-style composition in his major orchestral work, *Tabuh-Tabuhan* of 1936. Affinities with Grainger's much-earlier music for tuneful percussion are patent, while McPhee's next work, after *Tabuh-Tabuhan*, is Grainger-affiliated in that, called *A Sea Shanty Suite* and scored for baritone solo, male chorus, two pianos, and two sets of timpani, it involves a Grainger-style combo in something analogous to his ritual action-music, albeit without the Grainger common touch. It's worth mentioning that in 1935 Percy dished up Josef Yasser's transcription of a 'Chinese melody' as a pentatonically black-noted piano piece: a venture which may have encouraged him to embark, in the following year, on his own transcriptions of Balinese gamelan for modern 'tuneful percussion'. Along with McPhee's work, these had some impact on a major composer, Benjamin Britten, when he wrote his ballet *The Prince of the Pagodas*. Later, Britten was to visit Bali himself, with musical consequences audible in his church parables.

None the less, what Steve Reich dismissed as 'the old exoticism trip' was never Grainger's concern. For him, music was a way of life, or rather many ways which we will appreciate only when we 'Let all the World hear all the World's Music'. It didn't worry him that so epic an ambition might confuse rather than enrich us, since for him the social issues involved were important enough to oust fear. 'We see on all hands the victorious on-march of our ruthless Western civilization (so destructively intolerant in its colonial phase) and the distressing spectacle of the gentle but complex native arts wilting before its irresistible simplicity.' Irresistible it may have been, though crudity would seem a more appropriate word than simplicity; certainly Percy's own simplicity was at the opposite pole to the Western world's power-obsessed 'consciousness', and he was wise in believing that to save the world's music was really a 'green' act of *self*-preservation.

'Random Round', opening windows on to World Music seventy years ago, was the most historically significant aspect of Grainger's experimentalism, in tune with his conception of his music as activity and 'play'. His main preoccupation during his final years became, however, yet more basic, for he returned to the confrontation between music and Nature that had obsessed him as a child, and had triggered his teenage creation of the *Hill Songs*. During his brief tenureship of the chair of the Music Department at New York University's College of Fine Arts, Grainger outlined the proposed course of study in these words:

The main purpose of this course is to make the student so familiar with the chief types of music of all periods and places (in so far as they are known and available), to show the threads of unity running through all kinds of music (Primitive music, folksong, jazz, Oriental and Western art-music) and to point out the apparent goal of all musical progress (increasing discordance, ever closer intervals and the growing use of sliding tones without fixed pitch, growing informality of musical form, irregular rhythms making towards 'beatless music')—until finally 'Free Music' is reached, when music will be technically advanced enough to tally the irregularity, subtlety and complexity of life and nature—including human nature.

As a model for human advancement that seems a tall, and probably unrealizable, order: which is probably why Grainger's doctrine of Free Music got entangled with some of his crankier formulations. In one of his broadcast lectures, given in the same year as his address to the College of Fine Arts, Grainger opines that the Ultimate Goal of Human Progress, Free Music, will also be

the fullest musical expression of the scientific Nature-worship begun by the Greeks and carried forward by the Nordic Races. It will be the musical counterpart of Nordic pioneering, athleticism, nudism. In all respects it will be cosmic and impersonal, differentiated from the strongly personal and 'dramatic' notion of non-Nordic Europe with its emphasis on sex, possession, ambition, jealousy, and strife.

That somewhat lunatic prognostication seems a far cry from the Grainger whose highest virtue was personality democratically directed. But it should not encourage us to side with those who maintained that Grainger, fiddling with his machines at White Plains, was relapsing into senile debility, if not dementia; for his musical, as distinct from his 'cosmic', purpose remained consistent with his ideals since early youth. Burnett Cross, a physicist who became Grainger's technical assistant and valued friend, explained in a broadcast interview in 1966 that Percy hadn't wanted 'to be limited to the pitch of the ordinary scale or any fraction of any known scale. He wanted to be able to select any pitch he pleased', as was theoretically possible on a stringed instrument or a trombone. Only it was not merely a matter of wanting to go from one tone to another by

a glide rather than by a hop; it was also a matter of being able to control the precise slope and duration of that glide . . . So the first experiments we tried were completely mechanical, adapting principles from the pianola and the Duo-Art machine. [In the end, however, they became] almost completely electronic . . . I think we were as electronic as we could get because all that remained of the mechanical business was the graphs on a roll of clear plastic which moved from one point to another across a system of photo-cells . . . The machine that we were working on when Percy died was to have seven voices, and that meant that it had, that it played from, fourteen graphs, two graphs for each voice, one for the pitch and one, a smaller one, for the dynamics . . . The machines that we made showed, to my surprise, that they could be adjusted to play more, with more precision, than a human performer could!

This was a further aim of Grainger's Free Music: to eliminate the human performer, not because music was or ought to be inhuman, but because a performer, being a fallible intermediary between a composer and the sounds he imagined, must distort. Burnett Cross waxed lyrical when these graphs of brown paper inserted in this 'weird mechanical contraption' began to make music with 'far more expression and dynamic control than any pianola that was ever built. I shouldn't have been surprised, but I was taken aback. I wasn't prepared for that.'

But Grainger was, having notated on graphs the sounds he wanted, certainly before 1930 and possibly, Burnett Cross hazards, before 1920. The technicalities involved in the Free Music machines are too abstruse to be explored in a book as small as this, and perhaps exploration would be unjustified in a study of Grainger's music, since virtually no compositions for the machines are extant. But Percy's own brief account of his intentions, written in 1938 and republished in Theresa Balough's *A Musical Genius from Australia*, should be considered: as should Richard Franko Goldman's article on 'Percy Grainger's Free Music', first published in the *Juillard Review* in 1955, and also reprinted in Teresa Balough's compilation. This is by far the most illuminating account of how the machines were supposed to work, its burden being that 'free' music as Grainger conceived it was free as to means but composed in its ends. The machines are essentially composing instruments which can 'write out' a simple four-part chorale or a vastly complex piece in graded microtonal intervals; 'in practice', Goldman writes,

someone completely unschooled might produce 'free music' experimentally, or by accident, without even attempting to imagine in advance what the resulting sound might be like: the purest kind of music is possible. But of course any end may also be accomplished by design, provided that the composer can really hear microtonal intervals, and can think in free rhythms.

Theoretically, it would therefore seem that Grainger's concept of Free Music could have made recordable, with calculated precision, all the instinctive vagaries of pitch and rhythm that he so admired in his folk-singers, and had tried to emulate through the crude means of conventional notation. Two questions remain unanswered. Why, if this is so, did Grainger's Free Music not become operative? And why did Percy not take full advantage of the resources of electrophonics as they became available? Burnett Cross, as we have noted, had some resort to electric techniques, and Grainger himself attended a lecture by Stockhausen in 1958, laconically commenting in his notebook with the single word: 'GOOD'. It would seem that Grainger's confusion came from the fact that he mistrusted the machines even as he admired them, fearing that scientific system might oust musical justification. Perhaps Percy's muddle-headedness was evidence of the soundness of his heart, for—despite the considerable achievements of electrophonic music thus far—its story has not been encouraging to those who feel, as did Percy, that music should inspire delight. One may now 'compose' at synthesizers in any preordained style or in none; but the fact that 'anyone' can do it, doesn't make what is done more worth the carrying. One begins to wonder whether Grainger's failure to carry through his scientific experiments to the bitter, or even the potentially sweet, end may not have been a saving grace. Dubiety would seem to be reflected in the fantastic names with which he christened his machines, some of them put together out of bits of junk such as milk-bottles, sewing-machines, drum-brakes, hair-dryers, pencil-sharpeners, and what-else. The names express a humorous wonderment at the audacity of the enterprises, but they certainly debunk the engines of pomposity; one cannot be very scared of, let alone awed by, an Inflated Frog Blower, a Crumb-Catcher and Drain-Protector Disc, not to mention a Cross-Grainger Double-Decker Kangaroo-Pouch Flying-Disc Paper Graph Model for Synchronizing and Playing 8 Oscillators. One is reminded of the Found Objects and junk percussion instruments assembled in the forties and fifties by John Cage and Lou Harrison, and still more of the beautiful, and beautifully named, instruments contemporaneously constructed by Harry Partch from the natural materials of his Californian environment. The difference is that Cage's and Harrison's instruments, all naturally acoustic, all worked; and that Partch's more elaborate instruments were likewise acoustic, completed, and playable, if difficult to store and maintain.

Richard Franko Goldman, author of the most informative discussion of Grainger's Free Music, was also a colleague of Percy's whilst he was involved in the American wind-band movement. It may be that the wise child Percy was increasingly aware of a disparity between that audible creation and the sonic theory which he couldn't, fun though he found it, bring to fruition. His riposte to the manifest imperfectability of life was to seek for acoustical perfection, whereby every infinitesimal gradation of pitch and rhythm would be precisely chartable. But his innovative role perhaps became increasingly speculative; though he enjoyed playing the games, he cared less and less whether they paid off. The 'hills themselves' would remain permanently unassailable; but in *A Lincolnshire Posy*, played by his friend Goldman, he could hear the Happy Tribes of Lincolnshire living, as had he, with irremediably imperfect but unbashed delight.

So at White Plains he could exclaim to Ella: 'O the joys of old age! Being able to work with my funny machines and doing other things one likes even if others do not think it worth while.' But still more 'soul-satisfying' was the fact that his published music, especially the wind-band music, could now be more frequently heard, expertly performed by the likes of Richard Franko Goldman. 'I am UTTERLY HAPPY in my now-time-y life', Grainger enthuses; 'I like to be kow-towed to & I like all the treatments that come to old age. Now that time-beaters and other tone-show planners know that I set store only by my tone-works & not by my piano playing, they try to be awfully nice to me about it . . . they really DO try to please and give me life-fulfilment.'

So perhaps we shouldn't regret that there was so little audible, as distinct from visible, return for Grainger's years of labour on the Free Music machines. Only two fragments of Free Music are extant: one a one-and-a-half minute 'sample' for six theremins (an early monophonic electronic instrument), the other a thirty-second snatch for microtonal 'string four-some'. Electronic realizations of these snippets have been made by Barry Conyngham, but this is a tiny harvest from so much application. One may goggle at the machines in the Grainger Museum, marvelling at their grotesquerie; but their stony silence depresses and disturbs. Their fate is far sadder than that of Harry Partch's instruments, since he left a core of notated music that needs them for its realization, and most of Partch's works have in fact been performed and recorded by a band of devoted disciples. Grainger, leaving virtually no Free Music, needed no disciples, and in this respect had none.

Did the Lonely Desert Man, closeted with his machines at White Plains, hope to see again, through Nature purified, the shining tents of the Lost Happy Tribes whose songs he, a Boy Eternal, still hoped to sing? Or did he realize that his relative content in old age was his re-cognition that his boyhood-frolicking in country gardens hadn't staled with the thud of the years? Is memory more important than innovation? Could he, whose genuine music had destroyed barriers between past and present, leave the future to take care of itself—as of course it always does, 'regardless'? It is pretty certain that we have lost no great music through Grainger's failure with the Free Music machines, and we cannot even be sure, given the story of electronic music thus far, that the questions Percy was asking during his old age were *worth* answering. One may however admit that, since democratic people must all be *in potentia* artists, they have to go on asking what Charles Ives called The Unanswered Question, undeterred by the fact that it is unanswered because it is unanswerable. Percy Grainger—not, like Ives, a New England transcendentalist, but an *homme moyen sensuel*, if also a *puer aeternatus*—befuddledly went on asking whilst fulfilling his destiny: which was to make and act music, and to stimulate making and acting in his fellow creatures. That is a lot to be grateful for.

# POSTLUDE

## Grainger as Green Man

If, at the end of this brief survey, we ask where Grainger stands in the story of music, we come back to the fact that he is unique; there is no composer with whom he may be profitably compared. He did not leave a body of 'works' to be evaluated alongside those of other composers. His original compositions, in the conventional sense, are few in number and, by the standards of the great masters, trivial in scope. Most of his work rehashes music by other people, whether they be the anonymous Folk or accredited composers of art-music; much of his best, even his most original, music is that which seems to be most dependent on others. Yet this is precisely the point: from the first years of the century Grainger demonstrated that the accepted view of the Artist was due for reappraisal, not because there can never be another Shakespeare or Beethoven, but because such are not the most urgent priority. Grainger reminds us, in the very music he re-created, that the Happy Tribes of the Folk sang and danced that they might have life more abundantly; in process he hints that such conditions might again be feasible. Reaffirming the values inherent in Unwritten Music, he speaks for the health of the minds and bodies of common folk. In that sense he was a green artist before greenness had been invented, or at least named.

But if Grainger's achievement is unique, it may be useful to consider it in relation to other composers who seem to share some common attitudes. In the course of the book we have naturally spoken of the qualities he found in the three composers he most loved, Bach, Delius, and Grieg. A more equivocal case is Busoni, from whom Percy had a few piano lessons, and to whom he played his *Hill Songs* in a piano version. In October 1909 he wrote to his mother that it was 'very clever' of Busoni to recognize that 'I had much temperament (in other words, immediate sensuous ecstasy) in my things', while at the same time having doubts about my 'primitive impulsiveness'. Although Grainger had, in his quixotic way, a brilliant head, he was essentially a man of heart whose 'people's music', embracing folk and pop tunes, eschewed formalism, let alone academic convention. Busoni, on the other hand, was formidably intellectual if not conventionally academic, and was fanatical in his 'rage for order'. Yet both men were, by opposite roots, innovators who Made It New, and were fascinated by experiment in tonality and metre. Both were virtuoso pianists, travelling the world, exhibiting themselves and also history, since both were indefatigable arrangers and presenters of other people's music.

Grainger and Busoni were temperamental opposites who respected but did not love one another: as Percy implicitly admitted when on 7 July 1907 he wrote to Rose that 'the night before last I dreamt Grieg was so loving and caressing to me, & last night I dreamt Busoni said: "Yes, now that Grieg's dead, & I can overlook his whole life's work, I can see that he is a genius after all". *I fear Busoni wouldn't say it, though*' (author's italics). In humanitarian concern and in technical enterprise Grainger may be more readily aligned with a slightly older contemporary from the New World, Charles Ives: for Ives, like Grainger, was a philosophical democrat who broke down barriers between the genres. Even so, the distance between Grainger and Ives is not much less than that between Grainger and Busoni, since Ives's concern with common humanity was far more specific, and less childish, than Grainger's. Ives was frequently inspired by childhood, but also inherited and revered the values of a New England community much preoccupied with un-Graingerish notions like conscience and guilt. Moreover, in being a Concord Transcendentalist, Ives was fundamentally a religious composer allied, as we noted, with Grainger's *bête noire*, Beethoven.

There is closer analogy between Grainger and another American of the same generation, Henry Cowell, an Irish-American son of self-styled 'philosophical anarchists' who eschewed formal education. Literally an American Boy in the Woods to complement Grainger's Boy in the Bush, Cowell indulged in sonorous experimentation with a battered upright piano he bought himself when he was 15. Percy too had virtually no systematic general education—a fact which bears on his inability to think straight, despite his brilliant flashes of intuitive intelligence. But Percy was at least musically educated, acquiring thereby his fine harmonic and contrapuntal technique: whereas Cowell, given an opportunity for formal training in the twenties, set little store by it but became a pioneer investigator of World Music—an inveterate picker-up of global orts and trifles. As might have been expected, Cowell and Grainger became acquainted, and for a brief period Cowell served as Percy's secretary. Yet although Grainger must have appreciated the importance of Cowell's internationalism in America's polyglot culture, the two men do not seem to have collaborated in their experimentation, even when their fields of enquiry overlapped. If Ives was too intellectual, philosophical, religious, and perhaps moral for Percy, Cowell may have seemed mere flotsam on the surface of things. Grainger had no deep roots in a specific community, as did Ives; but his commitment to British folk music was a rock to cling to, a heritage that he found still valid. Cowell, lacking that validity, perhaps wasn't, in this context, a good enough composer.

There are also parallels between Grainger and Harry Partch, whose Global Village art and philosophy imply, like Grainger's, aspirations to social regeneration. It is not clear how far Grainger was acquainted with Partch's work, which was more theoretical and less empirical than his own in that Partch made a notated music-theatre for professional performers, rather than ongoing material that amateurs could make use of. But Grainger would have understood Partch's view that equal temperament was a Fall from grace to disgrace, while just intonation was a blow for the common weal; and he would have approved of the message of Partch's American Musicals, which are parables about the nefariousness of industrial technocracy, and the duty of musicians to act as seers, shamans, and magicians—or even as clowns, bums, and hoboes—whose activities might heal. Both men succumbed in their last years to curmudgeonly grousing about the misunderstanding and neglect they thought they'd suffered from.

It is not clear, either, whether Percy knew the great Edgard Varèse, the French post-Debussyan composer who became an American citizen in 1916, just before Grainger. They had interests in common, for Varèse made a music founded on 'natural' laws such as those governing crystal and rock-formation, as well as on principles of architecture and mechanical engineering, in which he had been trained; he also tentatively explored electrophonics in evoking 'deserts' both in the world outside and within the mind. Varèse, however, was a major composer with a formidable intellect; although, lacking support and appreciation, he composed little, he left a core of masterworks with which Grainger couldn't compete, and probably wouldn't have wanted to, since he was a doer and activator rather than a maker of artefacts. But at least Percy's experiments pre-dated Varèse's compositions, which mostly belonged to New York of the 1920s. Grainger also pre-dated another adventurous composer, Conlon Nancarrow, who has only recently achieved belated recognition. In a letter dating as far back as 1914 Grainger claimed to have been the first to have composed music 'especially for the pianola, because I have written things that can ONLY be played on the mechanical piano and have nothing to do with ordinary pianos. They are brilliant and light-hearted.' The pianola studies of Conlon Nancarrow, written from the forties onwards, are far more complex than Grainger's, and although all are brilliant, some are far from light-hearted. Percy would have revelled in the jazzy and Latin-American-flavoured ones, but might have been suspicious of the abstract mathematics of the later studies.

One suspects that neither Varèse nor Nancarrow was easygoing enough for Grainger, who would have been, and perhaps was, more comfortable with the clown-saint, John Cage. He must surely have heard and delighted in Cage's quasi-Polynesian works for prepared paino, created during the forties and fifties; and he would have recognized Cage's Indeterminacy as heir to his Random Music. Grainger died before American Minimalism was fully under way, but his ghost may smile at the news that Steve Reich and Philip Glass have carried Minimalism into the universalism of mechanized pop. Another composer for many years associated with Cage is the Californian Lou Harrison, who throughout his life has sought an equilibrium between West and East. Grainger would appreciate that Harrison's 'long flow form' is, in Percy's sense, Bachian, and would enjoy his American gamelans that nurture spiritual revival in an industrially based New World. Harrison is an advocate of the Global Village even to the somewhat *demodé* point of espousing Esperanto as a universal language. His music works on behalf of a Pacific community in more than one sense, as is evident in his *Pacifica Rondo* of 1963, pointedly scored for a Youth Orchestra of both Western and Eastern instruments. Eternally youthful Percy would have relished that; still more would he have rejoiced in the beautiful Piano Concerto that Harrison composed in 1985 for Keith Jarrett, a musician who lives 'between' the worlds of art, jazz, and pop.

The grandly spacious first movement is Bachian in long flow form and consistency of figuration, while having relationships with the tuneful percussion of Balinese music, even adapting the tuning of the piano to a compromise between East and West. The equally long but corybantic second movement, 'Stampede', makes the link between Bachian continuity and 'primitive' fiesta—as observed by Grainger in his improvising Rarotongan polyphonists. The meditative slow movement is as linearly and harmonically pure as a New England folk-song, while the brief finale returns to the continuous present that is our everyday lives. Many aspects of Grainger's global empiricism are here collaged, as the Lonely Desert Man and the Happy Tribes are reunited in a music that *flows, sings, and dances,* undriven by the will and unbuffeted by aggressive intentionality.

Percy Grainger couldn't have written Beethoven's *Missa Solemnis* even if he had wanted to; nor, for that matter, could he have created the Bach *Matthew Passion* he so dearly loved. If we therefore conclude that he was debarred from the higher echelons of art, that is not to depreciate what he did, when he did it. Although in comparison with Ives he seems limited by his childishness, that limitation is also a strength: for whereas the 'difficulty' of Ives's music is evident in his technical disparities between ends and means, Grainger's music usually 'sounds' superbly, and is technically impeccable to the measure of his experience. It may even be that Grainger's life-enhancing qualities were inseparable from the frustrations he submitted himself to, for which his mother was ultimately responsible. She would not allow him to grow up, denied him the advantage of a formal education, sowed the seeds of his loonier delusions, destroyed his women. Everything he undertook was to some degree aborted. He played down, rather than up, his extraordinary talents as a pianist; he didn't follow through his pioneer work in folk music; he refused academic recognition, yet failed to carry to fruition the experimentalism of his last years. Yet if it seems that Rose, whom he loved to distraction, came near to breaking him, it was his failures that imbued him with the common touch. We love him because, although so much more talented than most people, he was endearing in his very insecurities. His childlike music tells us that the 'happiness' of the human tribe can only be an act of love. Whether his music makes us laugh or cry—and it does both—it generates love while acting and doing, and is fun while it lasts.

We have a desperate need for ludic composers, to convince us
that the togetherness of the human tribe may again be realizable.
Grainger knew that he was a tonic to a weary world, over which
the pall of human depravity now weighs even heavier than it did
thirty years ago when Grainger died. In a letter to Rose dated 7
September 1911, Percy rather startlingly described himself as 'the
strange reward for all the cruelty & injustice done to the poor and
the under-refined'—by which he presumably meant the materially
impoverished and the spiritually un-nourished, in an industrial,
soon-to-be-war-ravaged community. It could just be that Percy
Grainger was right, and that an as-yet unborn generation of composers may prove him so.

# APPENDIX I

*Grainger as Guiser: An Anthropological Note*

During this book we have frequently referred to Percy Grainger's relationship to the phenomenon known to folklorists as guising: most significantly when he transforms concert-music into 'ritual re-enactment', but also in pieces wherein he assumes the 'mask' of another composer. Further reflection on the implications of this may be rewarding.

The most famously familiar guisers in British rural life were the morris dancers especially active in ceremonies to welcome the New Year, though they figured in other ancestral rites, here and throughout Europe. Such rites precariously survive in a few remote places today, although, their meanings forgotten, they may now be staged more for the benefit of tourists than for the local inhabitants. Yet not so long ago—certainly in Hardy's day—the ceremonies preserved something of their mythical significance, and their sacred nature called for secrecy. This in turn involved disguise; most morris-dance teams dressed in outlandish costumes, usually indicating a pre-human relationship to bird or beast, or to a pre-Christian deity of the earth. The captain of the Bidford morris team, for instance, sported a fox-skin on his head, the red brush trailing behind, bouncing as he bounced. Most teams included a black-faced Fool or 'Dirty Bet'; and most mummers disguised their faces, either by blackening them, or by festooning them with paper. Disguise indicated that for the time being the dancers were 'beyond' their everyday selves, engaged in magical acts that could affect the community, whether by promoting fertility in folk or crops, or by warding off 'ghoulies and ghosties and things that go bump in the night'. The masks were supposed to be impenetrable; Jack Smith and Tom Jones were not identifiable, being momentarily creatures from mythological time, if not from Outer Space, which hadn't been invented. Of course there were specific historical connections: morris dances were so called because they pretended to be Moorish, 'reaching all back', as Hardy's John Durbeyfield put it, 'long before Oliver Grumble to the days of the Pagan Turks'. But any particular reference to historically and geographically remote infidels was less important than a relationship to generalized Dark Outsiders—who were also insiders in that they represent forces we're unwilling to own up to, except in brief moments of magical and often comic exorcism. The role of comic doctors in mumming plays parallels this: dire deaths occur which are true while they last, though they may be put to rights by the wish-fulfilment of a waved wand.

Puritan opposition to rural rites naturally became ferocious; as Philip Stubbes wrote of May Day ceremonies in his *Anatomy of Abuses* of 1583: 'For what clipping, what culling, what kissing and bussing, what smouching and slabbering one of another, is not practised everywher at these dauncings? All which, whether they blow up Venus' cole or not, who is so blind that seeth not?' Admittedly, the prose in which Stubbes gives vent to disapprobation is so lyrically and rhythmically ebullient that it reinforces, rather than stifles, the rites' function of psychological release. Percy Grainger, a fanatical anti-Puritan, had no doubt where he stood, and played the Fool, in relation to modern industrial technocracy, in precisely the same way as had the mummers in their bucolic society. He even swaggered in self-designed towelling clothing to which he had attached, by bits of string, an assortment of objects—pencils, erasers, knives—that might come in handy. His multi-faceted, multicoloured appearance startlingly resembled a morris dancer's, not because he was consciously dressing up in an antique mode, but because he was inventing practical garments appropriate to particular conditions. If people thought his garb grotesque, it may be that he was the therapeutic Fool, whereas they were just plain foolish. Again, Percy displays a childlike guilelessness; and it's worth remembering that still-surviving children's games incorporate legendary elements from ancient mumming plays. In singing and dancing games like 'Green gravel' and 'Wallflowers' adult love and death proleptically coexist, alongside white clowns and black devils. If Percy played a child's part in our battered technocracy, this called for energy such as no real child could summon up or cope with.

In this context we may hark back to a point made in connection with *Country Gardens*, the one Grainger piece that 'everyone' knows. It was originally conceived, we recall, for whistlers and a few instruments; and whistling—the emission of more-or-less pitched sounds by way of the expiration of breath through the orifice of the lips—has always been considered a humanly musical activity almost as 'natural' as the burbling of babes or the war-bling of birds. As one might expect, the Irish were partial to it, their wildly whistled tunes merging into a tradition of music for primitive pipes. We sometimes speak of 'whistling in the bath' as a metaphor for blithe insouciance; when we speak of 'whistling in the dark' any insouciance involved would seem to be unfortunate. More probably, whistling in the dark implies an element of fright, reminding us that some primitive peoples regarded whistling as a slightly sinister—devil- rather than god-inspired—activity. Either way, there is no doubt about whistling's magical properties; and one might almost encapsulate Grainger's sociological, anthropo-logical, and psychological role in saying that he exhorts us to whistle along with him—in sheer *joie de vivre* and, *at the same time*, in terror. We pointed out that Percy considered it odd that people believed his music to be habitually jolly; he knew that while the guiser's capers may be as merry as mindless bird or beast, his black mask shrouds mysteries darkly untold, and per-haps untellable. Come to think of it, this must be why Percy Grainger, whose art and psyche were inseparable, had to be so weird a geyser-guiser. God may work in a mysterious way; but he does occasionally perform his wonders.

# APPENDIX II

*Percy Grainger, William Barnes, and Blue-Eyed English*

Apart from the fact that he composed, or dished up, *Country Gardens*, the one thing everyone knows about Percy Grainger is that he wrote the directions on his music not in conventionalized Italian, but in very demotic English ('Louden lots' for molto crescendo, and so on). This accords with the informality of his temperament and is accepted by people who are unaware that for him 'blue-eyed English' was a matter of passionate principle. To restore Anglo-Saxon English was a blow against the domination of alien, especially Graeco-Roman, hegemonies, and was almost an assertion of democratic principle. If he sometimes had to compromise because his publishers insisted that some of his directives were unintelligible unless duplicated by the orthodox Italianate terminology, this in no way abated the fervour of his crusade for an English purged of corruptions. He tried to ban Italianate words not only from his music, but also from his letters, writings, and even conversation. The cause was hopeless yet not altogether absurd: as is evident if we relate Grainger's battle to another that had been waged, at the beginning of the nineteenth century, by an English poet who celebrated rural life in deepest Dorset.

William Barnes, who wrote verse most effectively in Dorsetshire dialect, was born in 1801 and died in 1886, creative to the last. The son of a small farmer of the Blackmore Vale, he left school at 13; yet educated himself to become a clerk, a reasonably successful visual artist as painter, engraver, and worker in woodcut, and a schoolmaster of exceptional ability and charisma. A 'natural' as a linguist, he was fluent in at least five languages, and had a working knowledge of Greek and Latin and about sixty other languages, including Manchu, Egyptian, Chinese, and several Polynesian tongues! Also a musician, he played four instruments, sang, and engaged in amateur composition. He wrote textbooks on art and architecture, on music, mathematics, and economics, on archaeology, geology, and genealogy, and on philology and linguistics. Although many of his pedagogical books stemmed from his activities as a teacher, he acquired an international reputation through his work in grammar, archaeology, and folklore. Since these multiple interests were for him evidence of the plurality of God's glory, it is not surprising that he also found time to study at Cambridge for a doctorate in divinity, and to become a village priest, serving the community with compassionate zeal.

Barnes published his first volume of verse in polite English in 1820, he being as old as the century. The lyrics are carefully crafted and delicately poised; not until twenty years later, however, did his talent ripen to discreet genius, in the first of his collections of *Poems of Rural Life in the Dorset Dialect*. In these verses 'speech was shapen of the breath-sound of speakers, for the ears of hearers, and not from speech-tokens (letters) in books'. Even so, the euphonious organization of the verses, giving the illusion of folk-like spontaneity, was cunningly contrived in reference to Barnes's deep philological studies of both European and Oriental languages; he worked hard to achieve a verse purporting to be by 'bookless and unwriting people' and anticipated Grainger in relating the blithe songfulness of his presumptive Dorset peasants to visceral body-music—'the steps of the dramatic dance, the steps of a march, or the stroke of oars, as in the Tonga songs of the kind called Towalo or paddle songs'. To recover Anglo-Saxon rudiments was to open rather than to close frontiers, hopefully deposing the Latinate diction of genteel society. 'Breath-sound' and 'speech-tokens' in the above quotation are Grainger-like 'blue-eyed English'; and many of Barnes's coinages are no less quaint than Percy's—for instance, 'soaksome' for bibulous, 'folkdom' for democracy, 'folk-wain' for omnibus. His technicalities, however, usually clarify: vowels are accurately described as 'freebreathings' as compared with consonants that are 'breath-pennings'; nouns *are* 'thing names', while verbs are 'time words'; syntax is 'thought wording', conjunctions are 'link words', adjectives are 'suchnesses'. 'Sound lore' is on the mark for acoustics, 'fore-elders' sound more humane than ancestors, and 'wort-lore' is livelier, as well as funnier, than abstract biology. In the Foresay (preface) to his *Outline of English Speech-Craft* of 1878 Barnes claims to be upholding 'our own strong old Anglo-Saxon speech and the ready teaching of it to purely *English* minds by their own tongue'. Hopkins appreciated this when he became the most radically *English* poet of the Victorian age, in the process adapting some of Barnes's technical devices to his own ends.

A technical parallel between Barnes and Grainger is palpable, and there is a certain consanguinity in their ranges of experience. Superficially, at least, both Barnes's Dorset verse and Grainger's music are of childlike immediacy; it's interesting that although Barnes was an exceptionally intelligent and aware person, compassionately concerned about land-enclosures and other consequences of the encroaching Industrial Revolution, he virtually ignored social issues in his Dorset verse, wherein he celebrated the old simplicities. Even so, Grainger and Barnes were as unlike as they were like one another. Barnes's language was indigenous to the community he belonged to, and he erred only in hoping, if not believing, that the purity of his English dialect might preserve, in the teeth of the oncoming storm, the human values it had stood for. He 'belonged' to Blakmore Vale (where he was born and spent his idyllic childhood), to Dorchester and Mere (where he worked as engraver and taught school, and where he married and raised a family), and to Winterbourne Came (where in his declining years he officiated as village priest). Grainger, on the other hand, knew his agrarian peasants through their music while having no roots in their world, or for that matter in anyone else's. Barnes's linguistic quest foundered on facts of social history; Grainger's was a slightly lunatic game which, like so much about Percy, may make us simultaneously laugh and cry.

Grainger did not set any of Barnes's verse and probably was not acquainted with it; had he been, he would surely have found it irresistible. Ralph Vaughan Williams, a decade senior to Grainger, did occasionally set Barnes, and in 'Linden Lea' created an Edwardian parlour song that became a household word, familiar in several kinds of parlour; many people still recognize the tune without being able to identify it or its composer. Masquerading as an Edwardian art-song with piano accompaniment, 'Linden Lea' has—though it is plain diatonic rather than modal—the pristine flavour of a genuine folk-song. Having heard it, one seems to have known it all one's life; it would seem that for the young Vaughan Williams, as for Barnes, art began as discovery of the values inherent in English rural life. Grainger, as a 'global' outsider, could not attain the instinctual identity that had made 'Linden Lea' a mini-miracle wherein worlds peasant and polite, rural and urban, were momentarily one. 'Linden Lea', however, remains a once-off; and Grainger's distance from his subject, his exuberant role-playing, mean that he is closer to us, for whom folklore can only be guising, as it was for him.

# SELECT BIBLIOGRAPHY

BALOUGH, TERESA (ed.), *A Musical Genius from Australia: Selected Writings by and about Percy Grainger*, Music Monograph 4 (University of Western Australia, 1982).

BLACKING, JOHN, *A Commonsense View of all Music: Reflections on Percy Grainger's Contribution to Ethnomusicology and Music Education* (Cambridge University Press, 1987).

BIRD, JOHN, *Percy Grainger* (Faber and Faber, 1982).

COVELL, ROGER, *Australia's Music: Themes of a New Society* (Sun Books, Melbourne, 1967).

DREYFUS, KAY (ed.), *The Farthest North of Humanness: Letters of Percy Grainger 1901–1914* (Macmillan, 1985).

RADIC, THERESE, *A Whip Round for Percy Grainger* (Yackandahdah Playscripts, Victoria, 1980).

TALL, DAVID (ed.), *A Catalogue of the Music of Percy Grainger, with Biographical Notes by John Bird and by his Publisher, Alan Woolgar* (Schott, London, 1982).

# GENERAL INDEX

Albéniz, Isaac 4, 129, 142
*Album for the Young* (Schumann) 11
Alkan, Charles-Valentin 128
Amerindian music 134–7
*Appalachia* (Delius) 15
Arnold, Matthew 63

Bach, J. S. 8, 48–53, 61, 63, 79, 89, 93,
   105, 124–6, 129, 140, 150, 154
bagpipes 30
Balinese music 142–4, 154
Balogh, T. 146
Barnes, William 159–61
*Barrack Room Ballads* (Kipling) 26–7
Beecham, Sir Thomas 36, 44, 47, 69
Beethoven, L. van 4, 9, 50, 93, 150, 151
Bird, John 7, 11, 91
Brahms, Johannes 11
Britten, Benjamin 59, 81, 88, 143
Broadwood, Lucy 4, 66, 82
Bruckner, Anton 49
Byrd, William 123

Cage, John 141–2, 147, 153
*Central Park in the Dark* (Ives) 31
Chopin, Piano sonata in B minor, played
   by Grainger 132
Conyngham, Barry 148
Cook, Will Marion 60
Cowell, Henry 151–2
Cross, Burnett 145–6, 147

Debussy, Claude 4, 130
Delius, Frederick 8, 10, 14–15, 31–4, 48,
   65, 69, 72–3, 77, 80, 93, 96–7, 102, 123,
   127, 128, 129, 132, 150
Denmark and Danish folk music 91–8
Dowland, John 122, 123–4
Dreyfus, Kay 20
Dufay, G. 22
Dunstable, John 127

Ellington, Duke 8, 49
English Folksong Society 4
'Ethiopian' songs (Stephen Foster) 117–20

Faroe Islands music 88–9

Ferrabosco, Alfonso 122
fiddle music (Shetlands) 74–5
folk songs, nature and techniques of 73–5,
   107
Foster, Stephen 45, 115–20
'Free Music' 9, 10, 130, 144–9
Frescobaldi, Girolamo 104

Gardiner, Balfour 3, 128
Gershwin, George 127
Gilels, Emil 65
Ginsberg, Allen 8
'Global Village' 38, 118, 152, 153
Goldman, Richard Franko 43, 65, 147–8
Goosens, Eugene 128
Gottschalk, Louis–Moreau 60–1
Gouldthorpe, George 108
Grainger, John 2
Grainger, Percy (as pianist) 128–33 *see*
   INDEX OF WORKS
Grainger, Rose Aldridge 2–6, 16, 50, 92,
   93, 99, 154
Grieg, Edvard 4, 63–5, 68, 129, 133, 150
Guising (and morris dance) 156–7

Hardy, Thomas 156
harmonium 21
Harrison, Beatrice 14
Harrison, Lou 143, 147
Haydn, Joseph 4
Herrmann, Bernard 8
Holten, Karen 6–7, 15, 85–6, 91, 97
honky-tonk piano 61
*Housatonic at Stockbridge* (Ives) 31
Hughes, Dom Anselm 80, 123
Hunt, Alfred 80

*Ibéria* (Albéniz) 4
Ives, Charles 17, 29, 31, 36–7, 120, 149,
   151, 154

Jarrett, Keith 153
'Jeannie with the light brown hair' (Foster)
   116
Jenkins, John 122
Jones, Martin 59, 96–7, 125, 133

163

# INDEX OF WORKS

Percy Grainger, if not a great composer, was a phenomenon. A man of extraordinary charisma, he was at once a legendary virtuoso pianist, a composer of highly original music, an arranger and 'disher up' of folk music who pierced to the music's heart, and a figure of some historical significance in relation to ethnomusicology and music education.

This book is a study of the music of this paradoxical figure. It looks at the musical influence on his compositions of folk-song and of Grieg, and of those apparent polar opposites, Delius and Bach. It examines some of his more significant pieces in detail; considers his work in recreating traditional material and the music of others; sees him as a champion and transcriber of what is now known as Early Music; and looks at his sometimes alarmingly eccentric notions as to music's nature and purpose.

Overriding barriers between art, folk, and pop music, Grainger is difficult to categorize, and may be, in the story of music, unique. Ultimately, his importance may lie in what he suggests about the potential functions of music in a rapidly changing world.

*Other books in this series*

**Sweelinck**
Frits Noske

**Berio**
David Osmond-Smith

**Marc-Antoine Charpentier**
H. Wiley Hitchcock

**Villa-Lobos**
Simon Wright

**Wilfrid Mellers** is Emeritus Professor of Music, University of York. He has written extensively on music from the music of the baroque to the present day and on both classical and popular music. His previous publications include *François Couperin and the French Classical Tradition* (revised edition 1987), *Bach and the Dance of God* (1980), *Beethoven and the Voice of God* (1983), *Music in a New Found Land* (revised edition 1987), and *Vaughan Williams and the Vision of Albion* (1989). He has also been active as a composer and studied with Edmund Rubbra and Egon Wellesz.

*Cover illustration:* Percy Grainger, *c.*1904.

ISBN 0-19-816270-7

9 780198 162704

OXFORD UNIVERSITY PRESS